A WIDOW'S
SPIRITUAL JOURNEY

Prayers, Reflections, and Meditations
for the Everyday Catholic

Dianne G. Coyle

En Route Books & Media, LLC
St. Louis, MO

En Route Books and Media, LLC

5705 Rhodes Avenue

St. Louis, MO 63109

Contact us at contactus@enroutebooksandmedia.com

Cover credit: Sebastian Mahfood

ISBN-13: 978-1-956715-43-9

Library of Congress Control Number: 2022935993

Table of Contents

Preface

"Me, A Saint?"

Everyone loves and admires the saints. They were so heroic, brave, deeply in love with Jesus, able to live simple lives, and on and on the list goes. When we read about these heroes in heaven, and then read their lives, it is staggering to learn what difficulties they endured, how their faith was so deep and constant, and their abundance of virtues. That's when we think: "We will never get to be saints." Having pondered the rather extreme conditions between their lives and ours, I have wondered if these saints were striving to be saints. These days, I think not. Instead, they were intent on living their lives as fully in accordance with the kind of life Jesus wanted them to live, in the times and places in which they were placed.

St. Joan of Arc comes to mind. Here was a simple girl, uneducated, who heard the voice of God telling her to put on armor and lead an army. Any one of us today would immediately think we were hallucinating, but Joan lived a very quiet life and so was able to hear God's messengers. Rather than run away, she stepped forward to carry out the mission she was given. On her mind was the job of getting the right person crowned king of France. Becoming a saint was nowhere on her list of things to do.

If we look at the lives of any of the saints, I am sure we will not find one who on their own decided they would be a saint. Sainthood is not a career goal. Rather it comes about by living our lives in close proximity to the Eucharist and by being as attentive as possible to anything Jesus wishes of us.

Recently, a friend gave me a biography of St. Therese of Lisieux. Here was a girl who was the youngest and favorite of the family. She was indulged as a child, spoiled to a degree, but grew up in a faith-filled family. The death of her mother was a dreadful loss, but that is when she chose the Mother of God to be her mother. She is not the only person to do this. I have a friend who experienced the same loss and chose the Mother of God as her new mother. A reading of St. Therese's autobiography shows us that she was a normal child, but when her oldest sister left to enter a Carmelite convent, again she was shattered. In the final analysis, St. Therese and all her sisters entered the Carmelites, so their father, instead of looking forward to grandchildren, surrendered all his daughters to a hidden life with God. Of all the saints, St. Therese has become an all-time favorite because of the simple way she approached God. Her life in the convent was not one of ecstasies and other spiritual events. She was a simple girl who loved God very much.

Another simple girl was St. Bernadette Soubirous who spoke with the Mother of God at the cave of Massabielle in Lourdes, France. She patiently endured ridicule and all kinds of harassment, including health issues. Despite all that, she stuck to the story that she had heard the Blessed Mother talk to her. Eventually, the local priest had to believe her because she told him the "lady" said "I am the Immaculate Conception." The title was unknown to her, and she had no idea what it meant, but when she told this to the parish priest, he had to believe her because he knew of the doctrine which had only recently been promulgated. Bernadette's obedience to "the lady" brought many difficulties, but eventually she went to live with some nuns in a place far from her home. She never saw her family again. Did she think she would become a saint? No. Instead, she focused on doing the best she could while she was living with the nuns. When she died, at a young age, God gave her a special gift. Her body did not return to the earth as most everyone else. To this day, she looks like she is asleep and rests in a glass casket so everyone can see how beautiful she is. After she died, many people prayed to her asking for help, and their prayers were answered. Then, she was considered a possible saint. Later, after enough information was gathered, the church declared her a Saint, but as you can see, she never considered herself as very important.

St, Ignatius of Loyola had masculine dreams of royalty and of fighting enemies and conquering them. Did he dream of becoming a priest? Or a saint? No. When he was a young man, he preferred to dance with the ladies of the court and fight imaginary enemies. It took an injury in battle to sideline him, and during his time of recovery he read a great deal about the saints. When he recovered, he was a changed young man. Some of the things he did sounded very strange, but he felt a great desire to do penance for his sins. Along the way, he began to realize that God had a mission for him. Having turned from his ways of fun and social entertainment, St. Ignatius eventually founded the order of priests we know as the Jesuits.

There are countless people who have become saints. The one thing they all seem to have in common is that they felt led in a certain direction. Some women have become saints by reaching out to poor people, or the sick, or children who needed care and education. They were very dedicated to the causes which were simply an outreach of what Jesus has asked us to do in life – care for the sick, the poor, the needy, the homeless. There are several religious orders who were founded by people who eventually became saints. The one thing all the saints have in common is that they knew in some way that God had something for them to do in life, and they went ahead and did it.

Although she has not been declared a Saint, Mother Angelica, who founded EWTN, may one day be considered a saint. She started by doing programs on the radio. One day when she visited a television station and saw the satellite dishes, she decided she needed to have one, too. She never worried about the money because she was confident that if God wanted her to have a TV station, He would help make it happen – and He did, nearly 40 years ago now.

One of the things that I find most admirable with many

of the saints is how much they accomplished in their lives. Things that we might consider impossible all came together under their care. It did not always happen quickly, but eventually what God wanted came to be because of their obedience to His direction.

Listening to God is something that takes practice. We have so many things which can distract us, and it takes time and effort to learn how to be still and listen with our hearts. One place that is very helpful for listening is in a church when all is quiet – no Mass, nothing going on. One day, just go into your church and sit in a pew and look at the Tabernacle. It's hard to believe, but Jesus is really there, and He probably has been waiting for you to visit. In the silence, think about what you would like to tell Him. It can be anything that you might be having a problem with, or some difficulty with another person. Whatever it is, in the silence think of this and let Jesus know from your heart that you need His help. You may not get an answer, but some days later, you may find that in your mind, the difficulty has been resolved or that you've met that certain person and made a better relationship with them after having spent that time with Jesus.

We have all been given certain gifts from God to use in a way we must discover. It does not mean that these will be made manifest in a very clear way. Sometimes, it comes about almost by accident that you discover you have a certain ability which you had not realized before then. We may never know who the next saint in the church will be, but we can be

"everyday" saints by living the way Jesus asks us to live –
helping others, listening to people in need, and in countless
other ways. You may even be surprised to discover talents
which can help others in a way you least expected. We are not
here to be big-name sports stars, but we are to be lights to the
people we meet and offer hope to those whose lives are in
need of our help. Who knows? Perhaps someday, we will
think of your name and say to ourselves: Oh, they were such
a saint while they were with us. How wonderful that they are
now being recognized for all they gave to God and others.

"A WIDOW'S SPIRITUAL JOURNEY"

Dear gentle reader,

Today, you hold in your hands a small book that was forty years in the making. It has come out of the dusty journals of years gone by. Even to the author, there has been amazement that such words could have flowed through her pen. If the words herein provide you with comfort, inspiration, and hope, then the mission for which they were created has been served. May you be blessed and filled with peace.

About the author...................

The year was 1973, and a young mother was driving to New Jersey with her 9-month-old baby. The plan was to arrive in time for dinner with her mother. Her memory of this ride was forever emblazoned in her mind as she was driving through teaming rain along the Garden State Parkway. She was approaching an exit which would have taken her to her grandfather's house and felt an impulse to get off and visit. In her head, she argued that if she stopped for this visit, she would be late for dinner with her mother, so she drove on.

The next day she learned a lesson she never forgot. The phone rang at her mother's house, and she answered. It was her uncle calling to say that her grandfather had been found at the Motor Vehicle Inspection station and was taken to Rahway Hospital. When she got off the phone with her uncle, she told her mother that Grandpa had died. Then, confused, and unsure, because her uncle had not said that he died, she said that maybe she should call her mother's sister to be sure. The call was made, and her statement had been correct. Her grandfather had gone to the Motor Vehicle station, but the line was long. He pulled his car into the shade of a tree and parked. After a while, one of the Motor Vehicle inspectors noticed the car was still there, so he went to check on the driver. Sadly, the driver had passed away.

In all my Catholic upbringing, no one ever mentioned that we should be attuned to such things as an unexpected (actually, Spirit-driven) thought. Since then, I have learned this is one way the Holy Spirit works. It is my hope that sharing this experience will help readers understand some things which they may have experienced in their lives and mused about for some time, trying to understand what it was all about. In short, these are most likely the kinds of things that happen when the Spirit moves within us.

Included along the way are reflections which also were influenced by the Holy Spirit. The majority of these writings were spontaneous and unplanned.

Everyone's relationship to God is unique. No two are the same. Just as we are all created with different capabilities and personalities, we are wise to not try to create an image of Jesus. We will come to know Him as He reveals himself to us.

Writing was an automatic response to prayer, quiet, and silent reflection. It is not usually planned the way one would write a treatise or give a talk. In our innermost being, the Spirit of God resides, and it takes real, undistracted silence to hear His voice and to allow His Spirit to move us, inspire us, and encourage us.

It is my hope that at least some of the material included here will help you understand better how the inner life of the Spirit of God leads us in many different and beautiful ways.

††††

The Author's JOURNEY

It all began without a plan and in the midst of great pain. Death, even expected, never comes with an announcement of a specific date or time. And so, it was. On the day before Thanksgiving, a young oncologist struggled to tell my husband and me that his cancer was aggressive and that his life expectancy was perhaps a year and a half at the most. Before the doctor ever said a word, we both knew what he was struggling to say. We accepted the sentence. Neither of us knew that day would come in 6 very short weeks. The good news was that we had planned for this event, but we did not expect it to come so soon. We went home that day and sat in silence. There was nothing we could say to each other. The day came – January 9, 2008.

Afterwards, loneliness and a very broken heart. No family members seemed to care; they seemed to think of me as being strong and independent. How wrong they were. But it was not for me to grieve then since I had an important job. Quickly, all that was necessary was addressed, and I went back to work.

Working 60 hours a week was no picnic. I was tired – very tired. The one thing that kept me going was morning Mass. The Rosary and Eucharist were the most important part of my day. My prayers were cries to God, expressing the anguish of heart. I kept working because there was no other income. These were very dark days.

My favorite image of the Sacred Heart of Jesus heard a lot from me, but He was always silent. For those who know, a "dark night of the soul" had descended on me. God seemed to be deaf to my sorrow and my cries for help. There was no joy, no hope, no expectation of anything – just the daily squirrel cage of a job that demanded more than I could give. Over a year went by like that, and one day I heard a tiny whisper: "walk away." I did.

Now I had no job, no income, and no idea what would happen next. I had become totally dependent on God to help me through this. Little by little, things happened which showed me God was with me, and I began to breathe again. During this time, I began to keep a journal. It took more than two full years and a lot of ink to work through the darkness which surrounded me at the death of my husband. One day during this time, I decided to have a talk with Jesus. I looked at His picture and told Him I could never love again, unless He helped me to love. I told him that despite all the emptiness I felt I would still love Him – I would still be faithful. It was a real struggle, but finally it was a deliberate act of the will.

Being unemployed opened a new door. It was a door to solitude and prayer. I began to pray more often. The sound of the television became too much noise after a while, so I stopped watching. More and more, I was being drawn into a silence which was peaceful, and in that silence, I began to listen. I found the freedom to go to morning Mass without having to rush off somewhere else. I found great strength through the Eucharist. Little by little, something began to move within me, drawing me more deeply toward Christ.

By going to morning Mass, and now not working, I was asked to lead the recitation of the Rosary one morning. That eventually became a different role – one of assuring that we had different Rosary leaders for every day of the week. One day we needed a lector for morning Mass. I had served as lector at weekend Mass years before, so this ministry was easy for me to do.

Then, I was scheduled to read once a month. As time went on and I became more familiar with our morning Mass "family," I was told that one of our weekday altar servers wished to "retire" and was asked if I would be willing to learn how to serve the Mass. I learned, and my spiritual life deepened. Being in the sanctuary with the celebrant gives one a whole new perspective on the celebration of the Eucharist.

The church activities made my days brighter and easier to handle. Then came the day my dear neighbor, who was a Eucharistic Minister, asked me to consider serving in that capacity. She was gently but firmly persuasive, and I finally said yes. Of course, there was training which needed to be done, and more things to learn prior to being commissioned. This was a big step forward in ministry, but the day came and with it a surprise. After the Mass, one of our deacons had an "assignment" for me. A very sick parishioner needed some-one to bring Holy Communion. I was appointed – the newest member of our Eucharistic Ministers. The grace of God stepped in. I did the visit; cared for the person in need, and that began a new phase of my life. I have continued to serve the church in this capacity ever since then.

Each one of these progressions came so gently and easily that I did not realize they were the unfolding of what I had written in my journal – that God wanted me to be free to serve Him in ministry. None of the entries mentioned which ministry – just ministry in general. As I write this, I look back and see how very gently I was moved from one step to another in service to the church. Through it all the pain of my loss decreased. I became focused outward, not inward as I had been at first. Each time I was asked to do something new, it was easy to say yes. It has taken years to realize that God was moving me along at each step and turning my great sorrow into compassion for others. I could not see it at the time. It was only when I stopped and looked back that I could see the hand of God was holding mine all the time. The journey has not ended. It continues to unfold with each passing day.

FROM THERE TO HERE

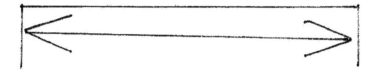

Every life is a journey. Sometimes, we have an idea which direction we wish to go in, and other times, we have no idea at all. The surprising thing is when we discover we have made a journey we knew nothing about and had no plan to take – not even a thought in that direction. It is only in hindsight that we can look at the path behind us.

Growing up in a relatively large family of six children, and being the eldest, I learned many things over those years. We were a family that prayed together and played together. The last of the six was born after I was out of high school and working. As a result, I had the opportunity to learn infant and childcare at a young age. Who would have guessed that I would need that kind of training several years later, but I did. When my own child was born, I was very grateful that I had younger siblings who taught me what it is like to care for a baby.

After high school, I worked for a while to earn the money needed to attend a school in New York City. I did well with the company, but the personnel manager was not happy when I left to continue my education. I think they had plans for me which I foiled. However, it is not too often that a company comes across a 17-year-old kid who can put together a training manual for a department.

The school in New York prepared me to work in corporate offices at the executive level. It was demanding not only in performance of our tasks, but also in terms of how we dressed. We were being trained for upper management assistance. However, upon completing my studies, my family moved further away from the big corporations. Finding a job in our new locale was difficult. Eventually, I went to work for the same company my father worked for – a division of AT&T. It was a good job, and I liked what I was doing.

Eventually, I ended up living in Connecticut. It was difficult being away from my family. Soon, I found some "benefits" of living there. Being able to go to Mass in the morning was a source of strength and consolation. When a friend invited me to attend a talk given by Sister Charlotte of the Daughters of the Holy Spirit, it opened a door within me that I had never thought about. I had never met someone who was so energetically upbeat about the Catholic Faith. I looked forward to attending these talks. One day, on the drive home, I was stopped at a traffic light. Suddenly, I felt that I was an empty eggshell. It could almost be described as suddenly finding myself in the middle of a desert. It was very unsettling. Then, it got worse. As the light went green, in my mind I began to hear voices asking me about my faith.

Question, and I would answer. But the questions kept coming faster than I could answer. Now I was getting very concerned – not afraid, but definitely annoyed. When I got home, I called a friend and asked for prayers.

Kneeling beside my bed, Rosary in hand, I began to pray. I don't know how much longer the voices and questions continued, but soon they stopped. I sensed the presence of the Blessed Mother. I never said a word about how I was afraid of Jesus, but I held a view that He was unapproachable. This was my sense, but I also sensed the inner words of Our Lady: "Let me introduce you to my Son." With that, I seemed to meet Jesus and feel a sense of peace within me. All this experience was very new and strange to me. Fortunately, I had a Benedictine Uncle I could talk to, and he helped me realize that I had received a special grace. The experience was not something with which I was familiar. I suspect many Catholics do not know that things like this can happen when we decide we want to draw closer to Our Lord.

Subsequently, I found a Charismatic Renewal group in my town. Through those meetings, which were very power-ful, I started to develop a closer "walk" with Jesus. This group gathered about 300 people from around the area on a Thursday night. It was awe-inspiring to be with them as they began to pray, some in strange languages, and hear the voices rise and then suddenly fall silent. Someone might stand and share an inspiration from the Holy Spirit. Eventually, I went through the Life in the Spirit Seminar and began to understand that the prayers prayed are designed to release the activity of the Holy Spirit within us. From this release came gifts such as physical healing, and other signs of the miracles worked by Jesus. During this time, I was privileged to be the prayer partner of a priest who said a healing Mass for us. After the Mass, he and I prayed with the people as they came forward. We would place a hand on the person's head or shoulder as each one came forward. We prayed that God would grant them the healing they were seeking. One lady came forward who asked that her legs become the same length. It seems, she had one leg which was shorter than the other. Father asked her to wait until we had finished praying with everyone. When we were done, Father invited the woman to come into a smaller room and be seated in a chair. He held her feet at the heels, and my hands were mid-way above and below on her calves. In this position, we began to pray. Because of my desire to pray with all the strength I possessed, my eyes were closed as we asked God to heal this lady. While we were praying, I could feel her leg move. When the prayers were finished, the woman stood up, perfectly straight! God had answered our prayers.

One might think that being a part of such a tremendous healing, those of us who prayed would be exhilarated or at least excited. That was not the case. There was a peacefulness in us which rejoiced at the good work the Lord had done for this person. The gift of peacefulness made us very well aware that we were just intercessors and that the Lord Himself was the one who did the "work" which the person desired. We were merely witnesses.

Looking back at that time in my life, I can see that while I was participating in these prayers, the Lord was also teaching me lessons like compassion, patience, and trust among other gifts I received. What was most moving was the energy of that group of people. It was almost like being among the first believers in the early church.

Following this time of introduction to the power of the Holy Spirit and a deeper way of praying, I was relocated to another town. I had resisted the move for about a year, but one day prior to moving I visited the local church. I went to the ambo to read the reading for the day. This is what I saw: "Long have I waited for your coming."

After I moved into the new town, I went to another town for morning Mass. That morning the entrance hymn was: "Long have I waited for your coming." I concluded that this was where God wanted me after all. I've been here ever since then.

MARY'S INFLUENCE

The Mother of God is a special influence in my life. From early childhood, she began her role of "mothering" me, often through my Grandmother's taking me to Novenas on weekday nights. One of my fondest memories is of our family praying the Rosary together, particularly during Lent. As I grew up and took my place in the work-a-day world, I pretty much forgot about Mary. I was still going to church regularly, but my routine did not include any regular prayer time.

After my daughter was born, I began to realize my responsibility of being her first instructor in the faith. But how could I teach her unless I really believed all I had been taught. Did I believe? Did I believe with enough conviction that I would be willing to give my life for Christ? These questions demanded a lot of soul searching. They also brought out other questions. Who is Jesus? What did He mean to me? Realizing that I had not been living the life of a fully committed Christian and feeling that I was too much a sinner to approach Jesus, I turned, instead, to Mary. I began asking for her intercession – and her understanding. After all, Mary as a Mother would better understand the way this female was feeling.

During those agonizing and difficult early days of my "conversion of heart," it was Mary who taught me to slow down my prayers, to not rush through them. It was through the slower prayer that something "strange" happened. I began to experience my prayers as coming no longer from my head. Now they were coming from my heart. I began to feel for the first time in my whole life that my prayers were really being heard.

FINDING THE WAY

Every soul holds within it the seed which, when it sprouts, will seek the Son of God. Some seeds will sprout quickly, and others will take longer. It depends on many things such as the learning of faith, the existence of God, the way to "reach" God through prayer and worship. It depends on the desire of the soul to draw close to God. Some souls are like seeds in the Gospel story, falling on rocky ground, or among thorns, or on good ground. We "seeds" are influenced by our families and relatives whose faith is either shared with us, lukewarm, or else ignored. How we respond to the invitation to faith determines how quickly our souls will grow. Even with the most prayerful families as our "seedbed" there is no guarantee that we will grow very close to God. Any plant can easily be started in a protected environment. When that new plant is transplanted into another environment, its strength or weakness will be revealed. That does not mean the soul is lost. God can touch that soul at any moment. Sometimes those moments are in the midst of great darkness or sorrow. Tragedy stops us in our tracks. In the darkest of moments many people find God and learn that He has been there all the time.

Those whose faith is weak can be helped through the prayers of others whose faith is strong. Those who have fallen into the difficulties of drug addiction and alcoholism can be rescued. The history of the saints of the church shows us a great many ways in which God can reach down into a life that is despairing and bring it out into the sunshine of His Love.

For those who are struggling to find God, He can be found. You have only to be still and listen to your heart. If it is hurt, ask His healing; if it is lonely, ask Him to be with you. If your problems are large and overwhelming, not only ask His help, but ask Him to send someone to help you. God hears every prayer, spoken and unspoken.

We also have great resources at our fingertips. The Eternal Word Television Network (EWTN) has programming for everyone, as does their radio station. Closer to home, the priest at the local Catholic church would be more than happy to talk with you. There is nothing to fear.

One of the first steps you can take on your own is to pray – whatever prayers you may know, or prayers you make up based on your needs. These are your way of literally crying out to God. He will hear you, but you cannot anticipate in what way He will respond. Our God is sometimes the God of surprises.

As children we are taught about God and the church. As we grow older, we develop a way of being in touch with God, such as weekly or even daily Mass. Beginners can use whatever prayers most touch their heart, but as they grow (through reading the lives of the saints or other spiritual reading), a deepening of awareness can often occur which then leads the person to a different aspect of the spiritual life. We tend to think of a life in God as either active (involved within the parish) or contemplative, that is removed from the world. Both forms of service are very ordinary. What many people are not aware of, however, is that when we make a decision to develop a better relationship with God, there is a good possibility that we will experience discouragement in one form or another. This is the first challenge, and it is one we will encounter along the road to a deeper prayer life and understanding what God wants from us. When this kind of confusion arises, the person would be wise to talk with his or her pastor or someone he or she knows who has been on the "journey to God" for a long time. Lay and religious people on the journey are good people to talk to. They can help you understand some of the ways you can deal with any negativity which may come our way – and it does.

And if all this is still too much for you, read on, and let the prayers that follow Peaks and Valleys touch your heart.

PEAKS AND VALLEYS

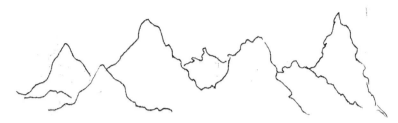

The searching heart seeks words of wisdom, words of consolation, words of hope. They may come in the midst of the darkest of times and the depths of loneliness. They may come through the words of others we know. In all the ways that are possible, they are frequently the words of God speaking to us through these various avenues. Even a book picked up and opened at random can speak of God to us. The soul longing for the comfort of knowing that God is alive aches for the consolation of God's loving presence. We know the comfort of a friend's consoling arm, and sometimes that helps, but in the depths of our being, we need more than that. We need the kind of comfort only God can give.

For most people, religion is based on the formulas of prayers and liturgy. Sometimes prayers like Novenas and Benediction come into play, but most of them are community prayers. Individual prayers seem to take a lesser place in our lives. The soul longing for a closer relationship with Jesus is usually drawn to more prayer – simple prayers, easy to repeat in a heartbeat. For most Catholics, our education in the faith ends with the Sacrament of Confirmation. We become young adults seeking to determine which profession in life will be ours. We become more socially involved, and the thought of prayer tends to fade from our consciousness. It may take years before we realize we need something more in our religious life than the practices we have been following. Reading the Spiritual Exercises of St. Ignatius of Loyola, for example, can help strengthen a person's faith and teach them about the peaks and valleys of the spiritual life. Once we learn that those moments, which prompt a greater awareness of the greatness of God, for example, creation, can be the beginning of a deeper walk with the God whom we cannot see. Truly, He is with us always, but we need to search for Him, and He will find us.

Once a routine in daily prayer has been established, the person may experience some beautiful moments in which God seems near. These are the times when we just want to be like Mary in the Gospel story of Mary and Martha. This Mary sat at Jesus' feet and drank in every word He said. Her sister, of course, was busy fixing dinner, so she did not sit at Jesus' feet that night.

As it happened, many years ago, my priest Uncle, came to visit. It was a late summer evening, and he was out on the deck with the rest of my family while I prepared dinner. That evening, both Mary and Martha were present to me. At first, it was Mary who greeted my Uncle. That evening there was an incredible sense of Jesus' presence in him. I (Mary) wanted to sit at his feet and drink in every word. Of course, dinner also needed to be prepared, and it was either I (Martha) fix dinner, or we would have nothing to eat. So, I was also in the kitchen – back and forth – indoors and outdoors. What a quandary! That night I began to really understand the roles of both these women. As is often the case, Mary is the example of the contemplative way of life, and Martha represents the active life – those of us who have a family to care for or are working full time. The great desire to sit at Jesus' feet was to drink at the wellsprings of eternal life. That night I managed to get a few "sips." On the other hand, Martha was the perfect hostess, preparing a memorable meal for all present. Her active service was a beautiful expression of the virtue of charity. Mary's gift was the recognition of the necessity of coming away from activity to the stillness in which we sense God's presence.

We had a lovely visit with my uncle, and I cherish this memory greatly. It was the last time I saw him alive. This was certainly a "peak" experience that evening.

Two months later, my Uncle died unexpectedly. Suddenly, we were all immersed in grief. It was the kind of grief that usually wraps itself around your soul and makes you feel you are in the greatest darkness in the world. All my family was immersed in this darkness – this deep valley of sadness. The October Saturday on which my Uncle died followed a few days of rain. That morning, however, the sun rose and made all the fall foliage glow. It was a brilliant morning – glorious. The beauty of that day was lost to everyone except me. The beauty of that morning made me understand that my Uncle's soul had taken flight in that glorious sunrise. Instead of grief and great sadness, as one would expect, I can only say I was wrapped in a "blanket" of protection. I was not sad. I could not cry, and it was very hard to explain this to anyone. While all my family was in the darkness of the valley of grief, I had been spared. Do not ask me why. I do not know. What is important to remember, however difficult a situation may be, is that in our lives there will be these peaks and valleys in our prayer life. While we would prefer to stay on the peaks, we must also travel through the valleys, which is why we call living here a valley of tears. It is when we are in those difficult valleys that God gives us the grace to work through it and by so doing become stronger. For those who have experienced these ups and downs in their prayers, they would be wise to find someone who is capable of walking with them on this journey, such as a spiritual director.

PRAYERS

Feast of St. Blaise

Several people and their needs were brought to my attention this day. The needs were great and prompted the following prayer:

Oh Jesus, spare us in our waywardness; spare us in our disillusionment, spare us when we turn to drugs and alcohol to deaden the emotional pain with which we suffer; spare us and give us strength when temptation presents its alluring and deceptive face; spare us when we become violent because of our addictions; spare us in our depression when we have no home, no job, no hope; For those who have asked for my prayers and other souls I have attempted to help – send a merciful smile upon them. Grant them the conversion of heart they so desperately need to see above the rut in which they find themselves; Save these souls and so many others like them who wander this earth in need of food, clothing and shelter, but most of all, Your healing. Fiat.

Teach me, Jesus

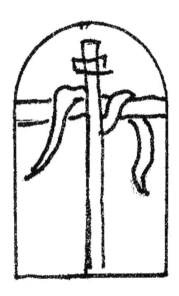

Teach me, Jesus, to listen for Your voice, or even just a whisper or breath. Make me so inwardly still always – even when I'm at church or working around the house. Recently, I have felt like St. Augustine, inwardly crying, 'Late have I loved You, O Beauty ever ancient, ever new.' Late have I loved You, my God. Draw me close to You. Cleanse me of my many faults, my lack of virtue, and all things which are unlike You Who are so pure and perfect -unapproachable Light. I now live for the Light and sometimes feel my being as light itself. Prepare me for the day I can cast off this earthly shell and can fly to You unencumbered and no longer dream of flying. Permeate my being with Your Presence and Your Peace. Amen.

Prayer at the End of the Day

Lord, all I ask is that You accept any good that was in my day and forget whatever was not pleasing to you.

A Prayer for Our Country

Heavenly Father, we come before You on our knees, seeking forgiveness for our sins and those of our country, our sins of murder, abortion, birth control, drugs, violence, hatred, animosity, derision, lies and all manner of evil not in keeping with the commandments You gave us. As with Abraham of old, whose intercession saved Lot and his family, so we beg You hear us Your children and save us from the evils which surround us. We are a country founded by faith-filled people who longed to serve You in religious freedom. Restore sacredness to our country, truth in all our words, respect, and love in all our actions, and Your peace in the hearts of all. We ask this in the Name of Jesus, Your Son, and His mother, Mary, our Queen. Amen.

A Prayer for our Priests

Oh Jesus, I entrust these beautiful priests to Your Most Sacred Heart. Share with them the secrets of Your Heart and draw them into an even deeper relationship with You. Grant them immersion in the well springs of Your Divine Mercy. Ravish their souls with a deep awareness of Your presence within them. Let them glory in the wonder of Your unfathomable love and be happily overwhelmed with the humility which comes from such an experience. Amen.

Prayer after Holy Communion

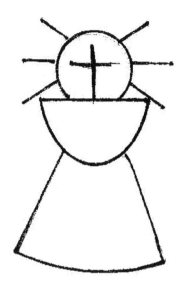

Lord Jesus, as I receive You and You come to be one with me, may I also become one with You. As You come to serve me, may I in turn serve You ~

May You become so present in me that You are truly present to others through me. ~

And as I serve my brothers and sisters, may I see it is You Whom I serve. Amen.

Prayer to St. Teresa of Avila

St. Teresa of Avila intercede for me. Of all the saints I have chosen you as my spiritual guide. Your writings have given me understanding and hope. You teach me the importance of humility and service for the love of God. Now, I beg of you, courage. As you well know, it takes much courage to relinquish all attachments in order to soar to God. Help me in my desire to love God so well that my soul is always on fire with great love for God and All. St. Teresa, pray for me. Amen.

All I ask

Lord, all I seek is Thee – to know Thee, to be one with Thee, to be inseparably united with Thee, to be lost in Thee forever.

Prayer to St. John Neumann

Blessed Bishop of Philadelphia, St. John Neumann, I dare to address you as my heavenly friend. Despite struggles and doubts which I understand, you remained steadfast in faith and prayer, in virtue and service. All these elements were like a gyroscope keeping you ever and surely on the path God chose for you.

It seems either you have drawn close to me, or I have drawn close to you. Either way you have touched my life profoundly and I am greatly humbled in your presence. Be now my guide and guardian that I, like you, may trod steadily and safely the path God has chosen for me. St. John Neumann pray for me. Amen.

A Prayer for the Homeless

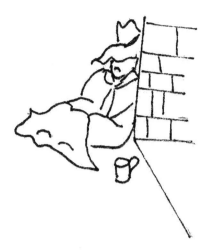

To the Madonna of the street –

I lay these souls at your feet - They are the poor. Alone, and homeless

Please ask Jesus them to bless

they that hide in tangled woods...................... and not in a glade

Of all things on earth they have no goods, nor work for them is made

The poorest of the poor they are, and see, those with wealth

Do not see them where they are. Yet I know they are there -

Faithful in their poverty - what little they have they share.

Oh, look upon them dearest Mother!

And see them round the manger in Bethlehem.

Draw these unlettered, unvarnished, into the land
Where peace and justice reigns. Amen.

A LITANY OF GLORY

All verses will begin with the following phrase:

Hail and Blessed be the Moment when..........

- The Virgin Mary was born
- The Virgin Mary offered her fiat to the angel
- The Virgin Mary received the overshadowing of the Holy Spirit
- The Son of God became incarnate in the womb of the Blessed Virgin Mary
- Elizabeth and the infant in her womb greeted the Blessed Virgin Mary who was carrying Jesus within her
- The Blessed Virgin saw her newborn Child and held Him in her arms
- Mary and Joseph fled to Egypt to save Jesus
- Mary and Joseph presented Jesus in the temple to Simeon who held the child Jesus in his arms and prophesied
- Mary and Joseph found Jesus among the learned men of the Temple
- Jesus returned from his sojourn in the wilderness

- Jesus was baptized by John
- At the wedding in Cana Mary urged Jesus to perform His first miracle
- Jesus walked the shores of Galilee and called His first apostles
- Jesus proclaimed the Beatitudes on the mountain side
- Jesus fed the multitude
- Jesus healed the leper
- Jesus raised the dead daughter of Jairus, and later Lazarus, and the son of the widow of Nain
- Jesus was transfigured before Peter, James, and John
- Jesus instituted the Holy Eucharist
- Jesus surrendered His life on Calvary
- (Pause)
- Jesus rose from the dead
- Jesus ascended into heaven
- Jesus sent the Holy Spirit upon the apostles
- The Blessed Virgin Mary was assumed into heaven.

THE ROSARY

This is a familiar prayer to many people. It does not matter when they learned these prayers, or if you have never heard of it before. The most important thing to know is that this is a very beloved prayer and has been in use for centuries. Through it, countless requests for help of many kinds have been granted. It is addressed to Mary, the Mother of Jesus, through a series of prayers said on linked beads. There are single beads on which the Our Father is prayed as well as the Glory Be, and groups of 10 beads on which the Hail Mary is repeated while meditating on some aspect of the life of Jesus. The "mysteries" or focus of the meditations is grouped into the following categories: The Joyful Mysteries, focusing on the birth of Christ; The Sorrowful Mysteries, which help us meditate on the sufferings and crucifixion of Christ; The Luminous Mysteries, which bring to our attention the public life of Christ through the institution of the Holy Eucharist, and the Glorious Mysteries which reflect on the Resurrection to the Assumption of Mary to heaven and her coronation.

There are many benefits to praying this prayer, including a deeper prayer life and increased devotion to the Eucharist. Through this prayer, many requests for help have been answered. It deepens our faith in Christ and his teachings. There are also promises from the Mother of God for those who make this prayer a daily habit. They are:

The 15 Promises of Mary to Those Who pray the Rosary

1. To all those who shall recite my Rosary devoutly, I promise my special protection and very great graces.

2. Those who shall persevere in the recitation of my Rosary will receive some signal grace.

3. The Rosary will be a very powerful armor against hell; it will destroy vice, deliver from sin and dispel heresy.

4. The Rosary will make virtue and good works flourish and will obtain for souls the most abundant Divine Mercies; it will substitute in hearts love of God for love of the world and elevate them to desire heavenly and eternal good. O. that souls would sanctify themselves by this means.

5. Those who trust themselves to me through the Rosary will not perish.

6. Those who shall recite my Rosary piously, considering its Mysteries, will not be overwhelmed by misfortune, nor die a bad death. The sinner will be converted; the just will grow in grace and become worthy of eternal life.

7. Those truly devoted to my Rosary will not die without the consolations of the Church or without grace.

8. Those who shall recite my Rosary will find during their life and at their death the light of God, the

fullness of His grace and will to share in the merits of the blessed.

9. I will deliver very promptly from Purgatory the souls devoted to my Rosary.

10. The true children of my Rosary will enjoy great glory in heaven.

11. What you shall ask through my Rosary you shall obtain.

12. Those who propagate my Rosary will obtain through me aid in all their necessities.

13. I have obtained from my Son that all confreres of the Rosary shall have for their brethren in life and death the saints of heaven.

14. Those who recite my Rosary faithfully are all my beloved children, the brothers and sisters of Jesus Christ.

15. Devotion to my Rosary is a great sign of predestination.

(Given to St. Dominic and Blessed Alan)
Imprimatur: Patrick J. Hayes, D.D. Archbishop of New York.

Note: Predestination is not a teaching of the Catholic Church. Since these promises were given by the Mother of God, they should be construed as meaning the individual might merit a special place in Heaven. Author.

Graces – most of the graces we receive through prayer or reception of the Holy Eucharist will come to us quietly. Often it will be a few days later that we recognize or learn that the prayer was answered. Sometimes the grace given will manifest itself in ways we do not expect, or we will become aware of the ability to do something or the desire to do something which we had not thought about previously. There is no outward sign with these graces.

Signal Graces: these are special graces granted to those who have been faithful to praying the Rosary daily. Our Lady promised to help those who show dedication to this prayer. It does not matter what the request is, She will intercede for us with Jesus. If the request is in keeping with God's Will, it is likely to be granted. But what makes these graces different from other graces? They are called "signal" because the recipient of these graces will recognize something special has been given them, either by an exterior or interior sign. The interior sign can be recognized by an awareness that the prayer has been answered, or a sense that all is well with regard to the request. These might be referred to as "intuitive" recognition because there is nothing outward that would give us a clue that the prayer has been answered, only a sense within that it has been answered. The person for whom the Rosary was prayed may contact the petitioner and tell them what has happened as an answer to their need. Other times there may be an external sign. A case in point was a lady who was praying for a friend's special intention. She did not know what it was, but she prayed. While on her way to visit this friend, in the winter, with her car windows closed, she experienced the surprising scent of roses. When she met her friend, she was told the prayer request had been answered. This is a clear example of a signal grace.

Another example of a signal grace is this: a woman was given a medal from a friend who had just returned from Medjugorje. She put it on her Rosary, and after a while all the silver links had turned a golden color. Her friend told her it was a message from the Blessed Mother to pray the Rosary more often.

MEDITATIONS

A Centering Prayer

This prayer is done in a quiet place where you won't be disturbed. Let your imagination bring these images to life. Then listen.

On the path – tall trees, but the trees become shrubs & open spaces, and the path goes on and on, twisting and turning somewhat. I run, then break into an opening. On my right small waves lap the shore. On my left, flowers are different shades but basically the same blossom, and there is not one bud or one dead flower. They're all perfectly open. Then I notice a bride & groom running down the beach toward me. When we meet, I discover it is Jesus and Mary! I hardly recognized them. Hugs and kisses all around.

Now questions come. Where am I? in the Father's garden. Mist rolls in. We sit on a rock-like bench. There is a small fire. I comment about the peak condition of the flowers. They are God's chosen. Am I here? I ask. Yes. What color am I? Pale pink. How do the flowers stay so perfect? The mist and the lake keep the right amount of moisture. The lake is spring-fed – no streams running into it.

I lean against Jesus. It's wonderful. Can I stay here? No, you have to go back. I notice statues in the garden – one of St. Therese, the others I can't make out. The statues represent the avenues by which people come to the Father. Jesus tells me I must go now. I don't want to go back alone. I ask him for an angel, and He gives me a very strong one – so strong he can pick me up! When he puts me down, we start walking back.

Now take time to immerse yourself in this scene and notice how you feel. Talk to Jesus the way I did and listen for His answers.

†††

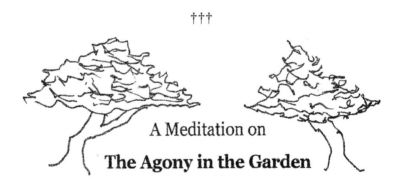

A Meditation on
The Agony in the Garden

The Agony in the garden begins, Lord, with Your arrival with the apostles in the Garden of Gethsemane. Then You, Peter, James, and John moved apart from the rest as they settled on the ground to sleep. You moved further away to kneel by a rock, but then Your anguished Face looked heavenward as You prayed to Your Father. The clouds parted to reveal all sort of evils that mankind has perpetrated on his brothers over the ages – and there in that depiction were the Twin Towers in New York, the children in Newtown, and many more modern horrors. It caused one to realize the enormity of the evil You saw that night – every evil act past, present, and future. These images shifted as the temple guards arrived and images of your arrest played out before me. In my mind's eye I see you being taken to the elders of the Jewish people and how they were relentless in their questioning. It is now late, and You are placed in a pit with ropes under your arms, holding you slightly above the dirt floor. You cannot rest. The long night finally comes to an end as dawn breaks above You. From here you are taken to Pilate, who turned out not to be sensitive to Your plight. For 'convenience' sake he releases a criminal instead of You, the innocent lamb. You have not eaten anything since the last supper; not even a drop of water has been given to You. But your sentence of death has a preliminary agony, a brutal, inhumane treatment which makes us shudder: You are scourged, beaten brutally, mocked, and made fun of by the guards who are permitted to utter every inhuman form of abuse at you, finishing off their most inhumane treatment of You by crowning You as "King of the Jews" with a tangle of thorns embedded in your skull. Watching this we realize that we have contributed to this "crown" by our thoughts, words, and actions.

Finally, You are presented to the crowds who are calling for Your death. The noise, the pulsating voices pound at Your already beaten body. Like fists hitting Your sacred being, the waves of sound from the angry mob assault You. There is no peace. Already exhausted, You are given a big, heavy cross to carry. The thought of that heavy weight on our shoulders causes us to shudder as we imagine how we would feel after being so brutally treated. Yet Jesus says not a word. Instead, He hugs the cross. Too weakened to carry it, and too heavy as well, Jesus struggles to drag it forward. Simon from Cyrene is pulled from the crowd to help You carry it. He is knowingly quiet, lest by protesting he would suffer the same fate. In my mind's eye I watch the slow climb to Calvary and hear the voices of the people on either side. I see Veronica reach out with a cloth to wipe your brutalized Face. At long last you reach Calvary and collapse on the ground, exhausted, and then nailed to the cross. Tonight, I see You stripped of all dignity, but when they take even Your loincloth, a gust of wind comes up and wraps itself around the cross and You and stayed there – a symbol of the Father's merciful love.

These images, not totally scriptural, but vivid, set the stage for us to begin to feel more deeply the depths of the love of Jesus for our salvation. Let us be moved to deeper contemplation and reflection in the next few quiet moments.

Concluding prayer: Oh Jesus, let me never complain about a few aches and pains when I consider Your sufferings

– all Your nerve endings on fire – enormous amounts of energy being spent by Your body, trying to stop the bleeding; not to mention the excruciating pain of every step when You carried that heavy cross. We recognize that the cross was very heavy, but to drag that weight after being so brutalized is beyond my comprehension – and then forgiving those who crucified You! All of this You endured to open the way to eternal life for me and so many others. It is no wonder Your Heart is so saddened by those who turn their backs on You.

†††

Looking Back

A Healing Meditation

In this meditation, we will begin with considering where we are today. Begin by placing yourself in a quiet place, either at home or preferably before the Blessed Sacrament, free from distractions, and slowly drift back through your life. Remember, all the good things that have happened over the years, as well as the bad things which have happened, should be allowed to come before our mind. As they slowly pass through our recollection, let us be aware of God's graces as they have appeared and helped us at various moments.

Remember the happy as well as the sad times, the losses of ones we loved, and allow them to resurface. As they do, ask the Lord for healing of those hurts. Not every day is a good day. Some days were difficult. Some people were hard to get along with. All these memories affect us spiritually in one way or another. Gradually let your thoughts slip back through the years. Pause at those points which were uncomfortable, or in which you felt hurt, and by whom. In this time of awareness of God's Presence, let Him heal those broken parts of your life, the attitudes which you may have carried forward unknowingly. All this quiet, reflective time is to be given to God who has watched over you all the while.

Let your memory slide back through your teens and childhood. Do not be afraid of some of your most painful memories. They cannot hurt you because you are in the presence of God who knows all things. Even the things of which we are ashamed or have tried not to bring to mind come to mind for the healing touch of God. Let them come forward now and present them to God for healing. Take as much time as you like and most of all give thanks for coming through these events and see the grace of God in areas of your life you would not have imagined.

Conclusion: As you come to the end of your looking back, give thanks for all the good things that have also happened in those years. Be grateful that we have such a loving and forgiving God and let Him hold you in His embrace, not just today, but always. Formulate your own prayer of thanksgiving.

HEART SONGS

The Meeting

A quiet walk, a bunny at play, an ancient gate that opened my way.

Worn blocks of stone, an old grassy knoll amid names now unknown.

I took a quiet stroll. Hallowed the ground wherein I stood, awed by this silence, I reverenced the good, the young and the old, those names of years long gone.

A great grandson remembered his ancestor in stone, but there stood I.

Among them comfortably alone. Each name I gently whispered, their lives now but a stone. I prayed the Lord remembered, and they rejoiced in a heavenly home. When was the name last hallowed, or whispered in tenderness? Who today cares to touch, the fragile stone with a caress?

Like old friends reacquainted, like new ones dearly welcomed, I touched and spoke and greeted some on gently bended knee. Here amidst passing autos these venerable ancestors rest - three hundred years are but a breath within the sands of time. So, as they silently welcomed me, I gently made them mine.

6/23/1985

Reflections of the past

Ancient tombstones with fading names breathe with the love of the people they recall. Walk among them gently they will tell you all. Lives left yet linger: they are still very much alive. They tell us who they were and how very well they lived, how tenderly they cared. Their epitaphs make them still real. Ursula left 4 sons, all in a row, Aged one and under if you must know. How great her sorrow must have been, but greater still was her love. Now they are all united in the One Lord above. If you would know the secret ways of living life the best, their lives are there still teaching in a graveyard we call rest. Walk among them if you dare. Gently touch and show you care. Their love arises like many doves. They're one united in the Lord of loves. Their lives still speak, so listen well, the way of life they silently tell.

June 25, 1983

Inspired by the music of Jonathan Livingston Seagull

Lord, may we go gently, all the Jonathan's among us, spreading our wings.

On the breath of Your love. Fragile and timid we are, but we are filled with that longing which draws us ever upward, ever outward, ever away from ourselves to be lost in You.

We will forget to be gentle. We may even forget this incredible, translucent, iridescent moment, but we are certain You will not forget us. You are our best Friend encouraging us to seek out our harbor of light, nudging us when we'd rather give up - always filling us with hope, and cherishing us no matter where we are. Our Faithful Friend, we've come apart to learn to soar -higher than Eagle's wings could take us – with our tiny little wings. Nothing tells us it is impossible for the call to fly shouts so loudly from the depths of our silence. You are our strength, You are our Source from which we spring, and the Port we seek. Look upon us dear Father. All we ask is that Your gaze fall upon us and we can see Your smile.

1983

†††

Grains of Wheat

We came as grains of wheat, tossed and blown in the winds of the world. We have been crushed, broken, and brought together in one loaf. Soon, we will be blessed and broken again, but this time we will be sent back into the world from whence we came to be Eucharist for all we meet. To sustain, encourage, and love to bring the Face of Jesus to our brothers and sisters.

1983

†††

Silence

In Silence, the earth slowly turns; In Silence, the sun slowly rises; In Silence, the clouds appear and roll away; In Silence, the rain falls until it meets the earth; In Silence, seeds sprout; In Silence, the plants put forth their leaves; In Silence, the earth hangs suspended in space; In Silence, all the stars and planets move and proclaim God's glory; In Silence, all the fish swim in the sea; In Silence, the doe walks through the forest; In Silence, man meets his God; In Silence, words are heard for every word needs silence around it.

The world says there is no God; but the world is full of noise; Man has become afraid of Silence, but it is in Silence where a man knows himself for who he truly is; In Silence, man comes to learn the true greatness of God. In Silence, our thoughts and prayers fly to you, Oh God; How marvelous You are that every prayer, every aspiration, every hope is heard by You. Jesus showed this to us when He walked the earth, reading the minds and hearts of all. He knows us better than we know ourselves – all in Silence.

In Silence, there is order; in Silence, there is peace.

7/9/2011

†††

January 2015

My soul sleeps like a sleep of death - all still, And so very silent. My lips speak words only the soul knows. They speak of anguish and of isolation. They speak in a deep silence - too deep for human speech. Great is the longing of my soul for the love of the Creator, but the silence continues .... Bereft is my spirit and my humanity, bereft of the trappings of this world. A sword had severed ties with the world and left me silent and very alone. Yet not alone, alone -but in the loneliness of a soul stripped of interest in the world...... Stripped of all desire for fame or wealth. This day I am reminded I wander this world a stranger – not to others, but to myself. My only joy comes through service to the homebound And bedridden. It is there that I find Christ – among the suffering and the child-like. My Lord and my God You have stripped me of attachments – the most recent being my loving dog – She who was there for me after my husband died. Now I am totally alone and vulnerable. Oh, God, have mercy on me!

Our Beloved Sheltie, 2002-2015

Weep for me no more. I did what I was born to do, to be with those who needed me especially those years with you. I could not ask for nicer folks Who loved me through and through, people who were warm and laughed at jokes, caring owners like your husband and you. You know I loved you when your husband died. I did not shed a tear; instead, I silently wept, and by you I was near. Together, we both learned to pick up and go on. I offered my lonely hours so you could learn again to be strong. And when my time came, you cared the most. It was not easy, that I know, but I left in peace so there would be no ghost. You asked that your husband meet me on the other side, and that was just the way it was when I laid down and died.

†††

Giving

A bright golden dandelion nodding gently in the breeze was plucked from its stem and given as a gift of love. After a while its petals wilted, and its color mellowed into a deeper gold. Still loved, the dandelion was placed on the table so it could be better preserved later. Though separated from its life-giving stalk though all its petals were wilted. The dandelion would not be thwarted in its ultimate purpose of revealing the totality of its giving of self to the world, for despite these obstacles it managed to produce the feathery wings for its many seeds beneath the golden canopy of its wilted petals before it completely expired.

†††

It is night

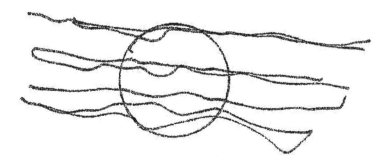

The darkness is illuminated by the delicate reflections of the moon on the snow sparkling like bright white fires. In the midst of a pure white field, the Lord of Creation lays His gems at my feet. Pure white snow - those saints in heaven now, brilliant gleaming stars in the field, those whose lives were shaped by His Divine Love into the perfection He desired through their loving, gentle submission to His Will. Like the stars which stand out in bold relief in a dark winter sky so, too, these Champions of the King stand out against the field of Light glimmering, sparkling, catching our eye and holding it for a moment. Beacons whose Joy is seeing the soldiers in battle find their way through – soldiers who find in them the strength and confidence to continue until we too join them and win the Crown of Victory.

†††

Raindrops and soft music

Flashes of white across the sky, rolling thunder rushes by. Alone in my reverie with my cup of tea, lost to the world am I and me. My soul responds to the Gentle, reaching, striving chords of music Straining upward, soaring aloft over the trees. Too much to do. Stop the world, it's going too fast! Are we victims of our own progress undoing ourselves by so much doing? Today is where yesterday just was, and tomorrow is fast on the heels of Now – too many yesterdays are giving me more of the past sooner than I want. The days come and go before I turn around, and before I know it, so many tomorrows are yesterdays of things I cannot recall. The drumbeats of today still echo in my ears, but the drums of each tomorrow are louder still, pressing onward I struggle, until the last mountain is reached, and I manage to climb to the top. There, before my eyes, is the eternal today sparkling and Glorious to behold. For all my efforts and pains, I have achieved that which I would not have believed even if told ahead of time Finally, I am free! I can breathe – pure air and I soar – with never a thought or a care for a backward glance!

†††

Lord Jesus, Thou art with me in all things I do this day. When I serve, You serve with me. when I love, You love with me. when I dress myself, You dress me, when I give, You give with me. When I receive, You receive with me. In whatever ways I go, in whatever things I may do, Thou art ever with me - beside me, near me, doing and being with me. How glorious shall this day be because Thou art fully in every minute.

†††

Inside a snowflake

Seemingly formless, and yet there is form. Seemingly disconnected, and yet connected, somewhat foggy and dull.

During a Snowstorm

Winter is a time for quiet. The deep snows would slow us down, cause us to stop, and see the beauty Our Creator makes for our eyes to behold: To surround us with so much of His pristine elegance that we are astounded to SILENCE, and quiet introspection, and the deepest Silence wherein we hear His Voice.

Oh Boundless Joy! For at His Word, He covers all the sins of the world.

And makes a new, pure, Virgin world. And in the snow, He calls US to be silent and learn the mysteries of the Universe and become one with His creation.

††††

Oh, REJOICE, REJOICE!!

The snow is a soft reminder that you, too, can be this easily restored to Your Father's house if you will but seek Me with hearts as pure as the snow I send to cover the earth. Oh children, even my tears become things of beauty to your mortal eyes! Can you see no farther? The snows of winter are a blessing and a promise – do not curse them. Know that even as countless as the flakes of snow shall be My blessings upon you if you will leave the sin and filth of your present life for the snows of My Love and forgiveness. My Love is Perfect as an undisturbed snow in an open meadow – faultless – flawless – gentle upon the ground, warming to the sleeping earth.

†††

The gifts of the Spirit should be yielded to when they are first noticed lest we deliberately thwart the Eternal Plan and incur God's wrath not just His displeasure.

†††

There is a way we can part the curtains and enter the Sanctuary.
It is Silence.

†††

In the midst of the praises of Your people You carry my soul aloft. You fill me with your love and Jo, and give me a taste of Heaven.

†††

You must learn to lean more heavily on Me.......... for I will sustain you.

There is much to be done, but you must totally abandon yourself to Me.

Only then will I be able to fully release my Spirit through you. You are learning even now of the Life in the Spirit.

†††

JEWELS FOR MY DAUGHTER

I send streaming from my treasure house, spilling over her and adorning her. Greed is nowhere to be seen. She responds with love, pure Love. Lord, where do you want these gifts? She asks. They are for you, His Majesty replies. No, not for me, she answers. They should go to Your other children - not me.

They are yours says the King. However, you choose to use them is for you to decide. Lord, I am not able to do that, the daughter laments, only Your Will can guide me. I resist Your love no longer. And the King smiles.

†††

The love that I have for my people is so great, says the Lord, that perfect satisfaction for their sins has been rendered because the greatness of their sins could never be atoned for through any action of their own. Therefore, I, Your God, have given you My Son in your human form to show you how great is my love for all of you and redeem you from your sins. Through Him you share My Divinity. In Him your sins are forgiven. With Him salvation and grace and eternity in Heaven are yours.

1978

†††

JOURNEY TO CALVARY

I'm on my way to Calvary. My own sweet cross I bear, and no matter how oft I fall, I'll not stop til there. For all the toil and all the care with life's each passing day is but a step closer along this passioned way. And so, my God, as I go through all that life must hold, I'll learn to love this firey cross 'til transformed pure like gold. I told You once I love You. I want to prove it, too. So, I'll join You on the Way of Sorrows and carry my cross with You.

Now when we come to Golgotha, Sweet Jesus, I know You'll lead to show me how to bear the pain – be stripped, and yes, to bleed. And even then we won't be done for then we've yet to die, but by Your side, my Lord, I'll commend my soul to God on high and following Your way of letting go for sinners, one and all. I'll yield my spirit to the Father, and then my head will fall.

1980

†††

POWER OF LOVE

Reach out to bless, oh, My child. They who curse and scorn others ask for their own destruction. They give the devil a weapon to use against themselves. I realize full well the world today is no easy place in which to live. That is why I insist that you keep your eyes on Me constantly. You cannot possibly love those who are in the world without My Love. You have come to Me, and I have taken you away from this painful place. I know how much you are feeling, and why you are feeling this way. Let Me fill you with My Love. It is indeed a shield and a buckler you those who put on My armor. I am beside you always.

1977

†††

THE CALL

Do you see, my child, how open you must be? Even with so great a friend and teachers as I have given you, diligence to My ways is of paramount importance. You see, hear, and feel parts of her struggle. How I have gifted you. I realize you fear you talk too much about these things and it causes you concern, but you must learn to yield even more to My love. I know you wish to be fully yielded to Me, but if it came too easily to you there would be no lesson to learn. How can you expect to serve Me if you Continue to work against me? True, you have fought My Love. But truer still is your quick realization of what you have done and that is why I have spared you from any pangs of guilt or remorse. Yes, you should rightly fear that I might withhold these favors especially if you would struggle with Me. Remember, I *will* not to conquer you. Rather, that you conquer yourself. In that shall be your crowning glory.

†††

STORM WINDS

The winds blew for hours, coming from all directions. The weathervane kept moving, undecided. Gratefully the house withstood the storm while it continued to rage. Finally, it was dusk. The howling winds fell silent, and the world slept

– at last. At dawn the morning star shone bright and clear in the stillness - its rays vivid and distinct, mesmerizing. Alone in the vast heavens beams clear, precise, unwavering - a reminder that hope is never lost, but springs eternal with each new morn. Songs of gratitude rise in my heart. In the silence strange sounds arise - generators – keeping water running and food cold. We have no generator – much will probably be lost. It is a sacrifice for souls. What better use can be made of that which seems a tragedy?

MORNING SONG

There'll come a day when Christ will come again. There'll be a day when the world will be at peace. There'll come a day when Christ our Victor King will give all hearts a new song to sing. Lift your hearts, be filled with hope. Let all our tears be now dry. All evil is on its slippery slope. Christ the Lord now fills the sky.

†††

A SONG OF LIFE AND DEATH

God calls a man to life, we know not how or why. He has to give himself.

And live only to die. We know not when it was that God at first began.

Because of His Great Love his history with man. We do know that He chose from all mankind one nation and sent His Word to them to bring them to salvation. He led this captive race from Egypt through the sea, and following His word, they were at last made free. And yet, to bring fulfillment to what He had begun, God sent among His people the God-man, His own Son. And now as God's new people, we are redeemed by Him Who died a bitter death to save the world from sin. We, too, like Him must suffer – He was God's Word made man – We too must lose our life to carry out God's plan. Christ gave His life for us, His Body is our Bread, And we who share His Life, will rise up from the dead.

REFLECTIONS

A Reflection on the Rosary

In the course of our lives, there are probably very few people who have not heard about an apparition of the Mother of God at some time. The ones which come to mind include Lourdes and Fatima, but also Guadalupe in Mexico, Knock in Ireland, Akita in Japan, LaSalette, and Rue de Bac, Paris, France, Medjugorje, and other places, but she has also appeared to many saints, including St. Catherine Laboure, through whom we have the Miraculous Medal, St. Bernadette Soubirous at Lourdes, the children of Fatima, Lucia, St. Jacinta and St. Francisco. In the majority of her apparitions, Mary has consistently asked us to pray the Rosary. Some people do not pray the Rosary for various reasons: it takes time (15 minutes), it is not something they grew up with, they are not familiar with the prayers, it doesn't happen in a group at their church, and other reasons. What they don't realize very often is that the prayer of the Rosary is like a highway to help us on our journey to eternal life. Through it Our Lady not only answers prayers, but She also dispenses heavenly graces to give us the strength we need to live good, holy lives.

Why does Mary consistently ask us to pray the Rosary? For one thing, these prayers invite us to reflect on the life of

Christ. They draw us closer to Jesus through her. Recognizing the difficulties in life these days, we need all the help we can get to bring peace and reconciliation to our country, and to the world. We need help to realize the difference between truth and lies. We need help to find peace in our own hearts. It is not just our country, but a great many countries around the world who need this help. Don't we all know, that when we need help, who is it we turn to?......our Mother.

Reflection on the Images of the Universe

As taken by the Hubbell Space Telescope

From the Psalms

Psalm 8, 34 I look up at Your heavens, made by Your fingers, at the moon and stars You set in place – ah, what is man that You should spare a thought for him, the son of man that You should care for him?

Psalm 14, 1 The fool says in his heart there is no God

Psalm 19 The heavens declare the glory of God, the vault of heaven proclaims His handiwork,

Psalm 29, 1 Pay tribute to Yahweh, you sons of God, give tribute to Yahweh of glory and power

Psalm 33, 6-9 By the word of Yahweh the heavens were made, their whole array by the breath of His mouth; He collects the ocean waters as though in a wineskin, He stores the deeps in cellars. Let the whole world fear Yahweh, let all who live on earth revere Him! He spoke, and it was created; he commanded, and there it stood.

Psalm 39, 5-6 Look, you have given me an inch or two of life, my life -span is nothing to You; each man that stands on the earth is only a puff of wind, every man that walks, only a shadow, and the wealth he amasses is only a puff of wind – he does not know who will take it next.

Psalm 75,1 We give thanks to you God, we give thanks as we invoke Your name, as we recount Your marvels.

Psalm 104, 1-2 Bless Yahweh, my soul. Yahweh my God, how great you are! Clothed in majesty and glory, wrapped in a robe of light!

19-21 You made the moon to tell the seasons, the sun knows when to set; you bring darkness on, night falls, all the forest animals come out; savage lions roaring for their prey, claiming their food from God.

Psalm 148 Let heaven praise Yahweh; praise him, heavenly heights, 1-2 praise him, all his angels, praise him, all his armies!

3-4 Praise him, sun and moon, praise him shining stars, praise him, highest heavens, and waters above the heavens!

†††

Fill me, Lord

Before Your Eucharistic Face, Lord, with In Sinu Jesu by my side, I reflect on the prayer at the bottom of page 281: "Fill me according to Thy desires not only for myself, but for others, for the souls Thou wilt send to me....."**

Later that day I received a call for assistance, and it seemed to be as if the morning prayer had been meant for me. Sometimes things are a coincidence, and other times, they are God's work. Therefore, it is for us to be open and responsive to any call we determine is from the Lord.

†††This prayer is taken from "In Sinu Jseu: When Heart Speaks to Heart: The journal of a Priest at Prayer by A Benedictine Monk. (Angelico Press, 2016) Thanks to Angelico Press for giving Permission.

†††

The Walk

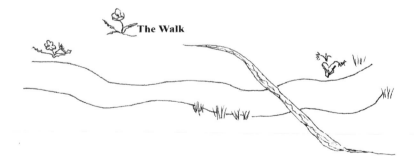

The Walk

My lover and I went for a walk. I picked a buttercup. "For the children to give their mother," he told me. We walked along the road and paused by the ever-running spring. I thought about crossing it. A little further up he showed me the way.

On the other side, up the hill we went. Then a path we found, and as I followed, I recalled the path of my centering prayer. Sure enough, we came to a clearing. Off to the left the ground continued to rise. Tall pine trees had laid a blanket of soft needles beneath my feet. I saw a large dead tree which had fallen, and my eyes passed beyond to an incredible rock wall. Nearer I came, climbing a rock here or there. One had steps built into it. Almost suddenly I stopped and stared.................... There was a break in the rock, chiseled so fine it reminded me of Easter Morning and Massabielle. I looked around this hidden park. If Jesus had walked out from behind a tree just then, I wouldn't have been surprised. A plant caught my eye, so I went to look. When I looked up at that great rock formation again, I could see a hidden recess unnoticeable from where I stood before. Logs in jumbled fashion like toothpicks lay at the base of this hidden place, and I dared not go further. It was a secret park with ferns looking like they'd been deliberately planted here and there. Further on we went, and I found a wonderful display of flowers – like yellow candles aflame, and I picked one to remind me this was not a dream. Had I died there, no one would have found me. It didn't matter.

Does God Speak?

God really does speak to us – in silence, in our hearts.

The Holy Spirit speaks to us in very important ways, if only we knew how to listen.

The road to the spiritual life is paved with the words and actions of Jesus which we are called to imitate.

The joy of life comes in the most surprising ways – if only we let Jesus lead us.

Reassured by a Peace the world cannot give, the greatest of joys comes in serving Jesus in others and discovering these words: "This is where I am supposed to be" accompanied by an inner joy no one else can understand.

The absolutely best freedom comes when we hear the words: "Go in peace, your sins are forgiven." Who wouldn't skip for joy at being released from the eternal chains for the sins we have committed? In our hearts, we skip like little lambs at play.

Even prayer takes us to a new understanding of our mystical connection with the unseen Creator, but whose Divine Presence we find in a spectacular sunrise, or the sound of the surf rolling in on a beach, or even the sight of snowflakes softly falling on a cold indifferent world.

Why, oh Lord, are we so slow to see and heart – only to realize we are seeking You and the peace of heart which comes only in silence?

How true Augustine spoke: Late have I loved You, oh Beauty every ancient, ever new! And yet all of this is only a beginning which opens onto eternity where there is no end to the joy and discovery of the infinite greatness of our Loving God. Who are we that You should plant this unspeakable longing in our hearts? Who are You Who would go so far as to become one of us and willingly die to show us there is more than just this life – and that it does not end but is transformed? Beyond that, we come forth from You. All of who we are is an unbelievable gift. And You endow us with a multitude of gifts, if only we take the time to discover them – grow in them – and use them to help us proclaim Your glory. Who could fail to rejoice in realizing that singing, dancing, drawing, painting, writing, and so much more are contained within ourselves? And as we grow into adulthood, the journey, the discovery, never ends. We are never too old, and it is never too late as long as we have life and breath.

Who will show us the way? Sages and saints, mystics and prophets still sing Your praises. Their words are still with us. We have only to look, and we will hear their voices.

Come, then, and let us sit in silence on a dark night, looking at the stars and hear the serenade of the universe, because it really sings!

†††

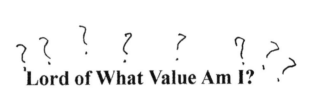

Lord of What Value Am I?

Tonight, I passed a cemetery and the countless tombstones made me think of all the souls who have come and gone – of the bodies that lived and died on this earth. And I asked myself – of what value am I? Of what value were those who have lived and died since Adam and Eve? Surely there is little value in being famous. After all, we can't all be famous. And some who were less famous and have their names on buildings, who really remembers them? Is it better to be insignificant? But, Lord, what value, what worth is there to a single human life?

Is it not enough for you to know that out of Love I created you? Out of Love, I placed you here to experience the world I created just for you. If I were to make only one person in the whole universe, it would be you. Not anyone else, just you.

For you are the Joy of My Life. You are filled with My Life, and yet I did not make you to be a puppet on strings. For my love for you is so great that you should be free. As free as I Am. But you insist on burdening yourself and wallow in self-pity and feelings of worthlessness. Oh, foolish child! All the riches of this world combined with all the riches of the universe cannot equal the value of you – all by yourself.

You are My Child. I have made you for no other purpose than to experience Me, know Me, and love Me. I am the Father who gently sets His child on the floor – Who holds His hands just a little distant so you can learn to walk. And when you learn to walk, you will finally run and find My arms enfolding you within My Heart.

Of what value are you? – just one little life? You are to Me My Source of Joy. To see you seeking Me, struggling to find Me, standing on your shaky feet, and finally running to My arms, is the Perfect Joy for a Father Who loves you so very much!

D.G. Coyle – 4/26/78

Footnote: Not long after "writing" this piece, I shared it at a Charismatic Prayer meeting. These meetings were large, close to 300 people on a given night. That night, after I shared this "spirit-led" question and it's answer, the prayers were followed by a typical "coffee and..." I had left the gathering and was in the foyer outside the chapel when a young man of about 14-15 years approached me. He said, "You know exactly how I feel." Surprised, I listened to what he next told me: "I have a dark secret." My reply was simply this – "Do you want to share it with me?" He answered, Yes. Then he told me about his difficulty sleeping because he was hearing voices telling him to do things he did not want to do. These voices were keeping him awake practically all night long.

Suspecting the cause of his problems, I invited him to enter the chapel with me. We stood in the sanctuary at the foot of the stairs, but close to the Tabernacle. Having been gifted with a new "prayer language" when I completed the Life in the Spirit Seminar, I began to pray as the Spirit led. I have no idea what the words were – they just flowed through me as I prayed with my hand on his head. He stood perfectly still but told me he felt cold. I continued praying, and he began to feel warmer and warmer. I don't know how long I prayed, but I continued until he told me he actually felt hot. Then, I stopped praying. The young man went home with his mother who had come with him. I never knew his name or hers, but it does not matter. Whatever it was, it seemed to have gone. As for myself, I went to find one of the priests who attended these meetings and explain to him what had happened. I was told that my response was appropriate and not to worry about it. And so it goes, when the Holy Spirit moves us.

†††

Confidence

I sit alone knowing nobody knows me like me. except God knows me. He sees through me, far beyond the facades I build for others to see. I tremble knowing that He knows me even better than I know myself. I am scared......I...... who will not face Myself, who look only into what areas I feel I want to probe, realize, keenly, that He Who made me knows the strength of every fiber of my structure, knows my weaknesses – all my failings, whether or not I admit them to myself. Consolation in the face of this realization is the saving, unbounded Love of My God, my Savoir, my Hope. He alone will never reveal to others my faults. Only to me. In this is my saving grace.

1977

And Suddenly – Silence

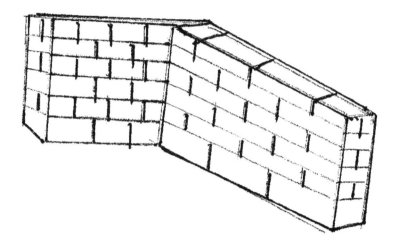

It was January 2nd, and the morning began with some sounds I had never heard before. My husband who had been able to walk a bit now found he could not take the next step. A call to the doctor was followed with a call for the ambulance. We went to the hospital emergency room, and before long he was taken for examination. The number of people in the ER grew and grew. There were so many patients they were lined up on gurneys in the hall. I stayed with my husband as long as I could, and then he was taken for X-rays or something. I did not see him again until late in the afternoon when they finally placed him in a room. I recognized it as a room for the terminally ill. That afternoon, he told me he could see the lighthouse in the bay. Everything seemed hopeful. The next day when I arrived, he told me there were devils in the room. I told him I would take care of them, and he became peaceful. I tried to be optimistic and spoke of our hope to once more visit Cape Cod. He wanted to come home immediately. No words could I speak. Six weeks had passed since we were told his illness was terminal, but the estimate of 6 months to a year had been far off the mark. That long day has now become a blur, but about 3 days later we were able to get him home. All the special equipment had been acquired, and the furniture all rearranged. It was the beginning of the end. He could no longer speak. His blue eyes were hidden behind closed eyelids.

On the morning of the third day, our doctor came. He was confident my husband would be with us a couple more days. That same morning, our pastor came, but I was in such a state I could not even pray with him. That same day, the hospice nurse arrived. It was a long, quiet day. Late in the afternoon, I asked the nurse if she wanted to see the tricks we had taught our Sheltie, Nikki. We walked into the dining room, and she did all of her tricks. She was such a wonderful companion. The nurse went back into the room where my husband was, and in a few minutes, she gently asked me to come in. He passed from our midst while we were out of the room – but his eyes were open. For the last time, I was able to look into those beautiful blue eyes, and then she closed them. I am confident someone called him by name. Suddenly, in silence, he slipped out of my life.

†††

Consolation

"Adoro te." "Oh, memories of the death of the Lord, living bread that gives life to man, allow me always to live for You, and allow me to taste Your sweetness always."

The sweetness You have shared with me beginning so many year ago, that comes and goes as You choose and with which You surprise me from time to time, Your Eucharistic Sweetness reminds me of the reality of this Sacrament. In the Eucharist I find not only Your Presence, but You feed me and give me strength to endure, to resist, and to be ever more devoted to You in the Eucharistic Species. Forgive me when words fail, and I lean on the writings of the saints. Forgive me if I forget who our celebrant is for Mass. One day is very much the same as another, except for some variations, but no matter what people may say, this world is very much a vale of tears. So, I must endure my exile here bravely while my eyes are fixed on life with You and the saints in the glory of the Eternal Kingdom.

Perhaps it is this longing for eternal life that makes me so aware of this vale of tears. Oh Lord, be merciful to me, a sinner.

†††

Simon

My name is Simon. I come from a dusty little town called Cyrene. It's not terribly far from Jerusalem. By trade, I'm a cart maker. On Friday, I was there with a new cart I'd made, hoping to get a good price for it from someone who'd gone there for Passover. I was in the process of bringing this cart into the city when one of the Roman guards grabbed me. I haven't done anything, I protested. No, you haven't, he said, but I need a man with strong arms and a strong back, and you look good enough. With that, he shoved me toward a man who was on the ground underneath a large cross. Right away, I knew where the Man and His cross were going. I've seen too much of the Roman brutality not to know. The Man could hardly get up and no wonder. His tunic was drenched with blood. What was strange was the mass of thorny branches roughly wound together on His head. Other than that, He looked just like so many of the other prisoners the Romans had executed lately.

The Man struggled to get up, and I reached down and lifted the cross. It was heavy. He reached up to put His arms around it, and together we started to walk again to Calvary. More than once He fell to the ground. He was so weak. I didn't think we'd make it, and I don't think the Roman guards thought so either. As we moved along, I realized that this man was no ordinary criminal. People called out to him – Jesus, Jesus! They called. Some mocked Him, saying things about His miracles and saving other people. I found it hard to believe this Man could have done anything like that. He seemed pretty ordinary.

As we continued our haltingly slow pace toward Calvary, He was stopped by a woman who handed him a towel to wipe His face. She was amazingly brave! I thought for sure the soldiers would have pulled her to one side. But no, they let her give Him the towel. You can imagine my surprise when I saw His face on the towel when He gave it back. I was beginning to think about this Man. Jesus? Wasn't He the prophet I'd heard about? Many people in town had heard of Him. I didn't pay much attention. I just kept to my work. So, I thought to myself, this is Jesus. This is the prophet and look at Him now! How much of a prophet could He be? Still, this Man who is barely alive, stopped to accept a gift of sorts from that woman. What kind of Man is this?

When we passed a group of women crying over Jesus, I thought they were all crazy. Then He turned to them and told them to cry for their sins – and the sins of their children. I had been reluctant to carry this cross, but those Romans don't take no for an answer. As we continued on our way, I became more and more amazed at His calmness, His quiet. The other prisoners were making lots of loud moans. They were snarling and saying words I did not understand. Every once in a while, the Romans would crack a whip to hurry us up. Jesus was moving as fast as He could, and I couldn't move any faster than Him.

When we finally got to Golgotha, my job was over. But I couldn't leave. Something had touched me deep inside as we made this climb to Skull Place. I had to stay and see what was going to happen. Then I heard Him say something as they were nailing His hands and feet. "Father, forgive them, they know not what they are doing," He said. I couldn't believe my ears. He was forgiving the very people who forced him to carry that cross up this long hill. When they raised the Cross and it slammed into the earth and stakes were hammered in around it, I thought for sure Jesus would scream in pain. But no, He didn't say anything!

Then it happened, Jesus looked at me. Despite all the pain He was suffering, I could hear His words in my head as loudly as if He had spoken them to the whole crowd. Thank you, He said. I nearly cried right then and there. I was speechless! Thank you, He said to me! No, I need to thank Him. He left the deepest peace in my soul and an understanding that my sins were forgiven.

I stayed all 3 hours while Jesus suffered that awful agony. I knew, somehow, He was there for me and everyone else. I'd completely forgotten about the new cart. It didn't matter. After He died, and the crowds dispersed, I was still there. I only knew I had just seen something very special. All sense of time had disappeared. His Mother was there, and after they had taken Him down and she was holding Him, I thought my own heart would break. I felt I'd just lost the dearest Friend in my life. Then, when they were ready to bury

Him, His Mother came over to me. "Thank you, she said. May there be many more like you who will help Him carry His cross." Then she asked my name: Simon, I stammered, from Cyrene. "You will not be forgotten," she said, and walked away.

2/27/2011

†††

Ministry and Mystery

Over time, the laity encounter priests, deacons, and nuns who have devoted their lives to Christ. In a family with religious vocations, one would expect that the person who decides to serve God in a dedicated religious life would be able to explain how they reached their decision. In asking this question, it is really not about making a decision, but rather, a recognition of being called to serve in a particular religious community or order of priests or brothers. The "call" is interior and cannot be specifically described in words. The best answer is usually that they have an inner conviction, a sense of knowing, and most of all, a peacefulness that assures them they can be confident about this inner tug at their heart.

While this may be a frequent experience of those called to serve God in a particular religious community, similarly laity can come to know a way to dedicate themselves as "laborers in the vineyard" in areas other than religious life.

For those seeking a deeper spiritual life, they may find themselves drawn to a religious community that offers a "third order" which will introduce them to practices of the religious order while they continue to work at their jobs. There are "third order" Franciscans, Dominicans, and other religious orders with programs for the laity. In Benedictine communities, laity who join them are called Oblates. Through these groups the laity can deepen their relationship with Christ according to the formula used by a particular religious community. Franciscans, for example, live by the rule established by St. Francis, while Dominicans follow the rule established by St. Dominic – and Carmelites follow a differing rule as do Benedictines, whose rule was established by St. Benedict.

Laity who belong to these groups do not wear habits. They retain their civilian lifestyle but learn from the charisms of the order with which they associate. The daily prayer routines of the orders help the laity decide which order they wish to join for their spiritual growth. One of the greatest benefits of belonging to a religious community as a lay person is the way our prayer life changes and deepens. Among the saints, we recall St. Rose of Lima who was a Third Order Dominican.

Many times, the lay members not only deepen their prayer life but also find themselves drawn to begin a ministry in their home parish. They might find themselves drawn to catechesis of the parish children or realize the need to start a meals to the home-bound ministry. Each person will benefit from their association with a religious community and from there reach out to others in need in a way similar to, or perhaps different from, their foundational community.

This is the mystery of God at work in our lives. One step in the direction of a deeper relationship with Christ can easily lead to other steps in a direction we might not have considered. The sure sign that the new direction we take, even if it was unplanned, is truly what God asks of us is the deep joy we find in responding to our own inner "call."

Lay "Priesthood"

Oh Lord, Your grace and mercy have attended me, and through my status as a single person, I am free to serve our priests and parishioners in a way I would not have imagined. You have given me the grace to lose myself in You so that You can reach my brothers and sisters. In losing myself in You and in service to my parish, I have found a great wellspring of love, and I delight in being an instrument through which You touch souls.

The card I received from a woman who survived a bad car accident hints at something more profound than she could verbalize, but I know that what she experienced through me was You touching her in the depths of her being. The laity may not be able to confect the Eucharist, or hear confessions, but You have called some of us to actively participate in the lay priesthood – being Your hands, eyes, feet, ears, love, and healing – bringing it wider into the world. You have allowed me to witness some powerful moments – sacred moments – with people.

In serving as an Extraordinary Minister of Holy Communion, we use the following prayer formulas: a penitential rite, we read the Gospel, offer prayers of petition, and lead those we are visiting in the Lamb of God, and the Our Father before presenting them with the Eucharist. We provide a time of silent prayer with our Eucharistic Lord after Communion and before we offer a closing prayer. We are those who bring Christ to others – the hands and feet which assist our priests.

More recently, I have attended the dying. Sacred time it is, aware of the loss the family members are about to experience. And there I stand, with them, knowing my own losses and how deep the pain. Yet, compassion and utter sensitivity rise within me – and we pray – together. The last thing the dying person hears is the melody of the prayers of those they have loved so much in life and who now give them the only gift they have left to give – their prayers. The passage is gentle and peaceful.

After I leave, I sense exhaustion. The heightened awareness of the moment and the oncoming sense of loss the family will experience all contribute to every fiber of my body being aware and attuned to the holiness, the sacredness, of these final moments. It is the best gift I can give them. The priesthood of the laity is a sacred trust, a calling to which we assent, and one in which we experience the closeness of Christ to those who are unable to be with us in the church. It is a ministry which calls for compassion and a heart attuned to the needs of the person(s) we visit. It is a recognition of the sacred duty we have been privileged to exercise as lay people.

When I am asked where my strength comes from, I say the Eucharist, because it is true. You, Lord, are the Vine, and I am a lowly branch. By being so connected to You I grow in so many ways: deeper love of You in the Liturgy; an increase in my prayerfulness; increased awareness of my faults and failings, but also increasing in some of the virtues, detecting and detesting sinful tendencies more quickly, caring more deeply, and on and on so that the glitter of this world seems so much rubbish and my thirst for heaven and You increases.

One very profound "ministry" happened when I, by the grace of God, learned that a person I had been visiting in a nursing home was transferred to a hospital, and then to hospice for his final hours. When I arrived, I could see notes from other people who had come to visit. Confident that the dying patient could still hear me, I told him I was there. At that late time in his life, he tried to respond. What could I do for this person who shared the journey of his life – from one end of the spectrum to the other – and who looked forward eagerly to my visits? Among my collection of prayers is a small set of prayers for the dying. I told him I would pray them for him and began to do so loud enough so he could hear my voice. I prayed through the prayers and watched and listened. There was no movement, no breath. This was a profound and extremely sacred moment. I waited. I watched the clock. A short while later someone came into the room, but they were not a nurse. I asked them to bring a nurse, and when she came, she made the pronouncement that he had passed. It was not his passing which moved me so much as the realization that I had been present at the birth of a soul into eternity. It was such a moving experience that I wrote about the deceased and my getting to know him. When there was a funeral service for him, I was invited to participate. The encounter and journey with this person truly was a sharing in the priesthood of our clergy. It was a gift from God Himself, and my reflection on this one life were the words I could share with all those who knew him and needed consoling.

✝✝✝

Holiness

Holiness is not easily achieved. The more one learns of You, our God, the more there is to know and love! St. Therese, the Little Flower, found the way to Your heart when she found a little violet, close to the earth, but perfectly formed. She found You when the hen gathered the chicks under her wing. She even found You while doing laundry! Help us find You most especially in those who hate. Help us to turn the other cheek when we are slapped. And help us to open our hearts more fully to You, the one and only Supreme Good.

††††

Trials

God never allows us to be tested beyond our strength: "testing makes for endurance" and "so run so as to win." As if that weren't enough, in St. Faustina's diary Jesus tells her: "All your adversaries will harm you only to the degree that I permit them to do so." Those are very comforting words. We need to be reminded of Jesus's words not just to Sister Faustina, but to us, when we are in the midst of life's trials. Life's difficulties are there to make us stronger, not to beat us down, and prayer brings us the strength to conquer.

††††

Ministry to the Dying

"With God all things are possible." If one is attuned to the movement of the Holy Spirit, it is amazing the things that happen in our lives. The following reflection was my first experience with a person who was not a family member. My first experience of being with a dying person was when my father was coming to the end of his journey and a battle with aggressive prostate cancer. When arranging for his hospice care I asked the nurse to provide me with some information on what to expect as a person departs this life. That information was greatly helpful to myself and my siblings because we had never experienced first-hand the death of a person up to that point. Little did I know then that it would be the first of several occasions when I was with a dying person. My first experience of being at the side of someone who was not a relative began with Bernie, whose story follows. After that you will find additional experiences which, like Bernie's story, were not planned parts of my life.

Journey with Bernie

A Reflection on the Life of BERNIE S. died 8/8/2014 - Feast of St. Dominic:

> *"As your hearts have been disposed to stray from God, turn now ten times the more to seek Him; for He who has brought disaster upon you will, in saving you, bring you back enduring joy." Baruch 4:28-29*

Bernie came into my life when he came to Madison House. He was in the recovery wing. The first day I brought him Communion was the beginning of a touching friendship. In reflecting on what he shared of his life, willingly admitting he didn't always live a model Christian life, I found not only humble repentance, but a life transformed. He was so anxious to make amends – to get well and to actively serve the God he came to know personally. He expressed the desire to become a Eucharistic Minister. What he may not have realized was that by enduring his sufferings to the best of his ability he was doing something greater – he was united with Christ crucified.

There was something sweet and endearing in Bernie. He may not have been a model of heroic virtue, but he reminded me of the saint who stole heaven when he was crucified beside Christ and whom Jesus promised would be with Him in Paradise. He also reminded me a bit of St. Augustine whose mother prayed for him for 30 years before his life turned around. Bernie dearly loved his mother, and I am sure she was praying from her place in Heaven. There's no doubt her prayers were answered.

Bernie had lots of friends as evidenced by the notes left at his bedside at Hospice. The day I visited him at Hospice was one I will never forget. When he heard my voice, he tried to speak to me. I sat next to the bed and reassured him that all would be well. With me was a little book of prayers, including some special ones to be said with a dying person. I told Bernice I was going to say these prayers for him. I began the prayers, and when I finished, I realized Bernie was quite still. In fact, he had ceased breathing. As I sat there in silent wonder at this gentle passing, I realized I had been given the gift of being with him for the birth of his soul into eternity. Bernie did not die alone; he died knowing he was loved by all of those who knew him.

Shortly before his death I was reminded of a beautiful analogy for our lives – as a tapestry. They are woven from the back and the image is not seen until it is finished. Each of his friends is a thread woven into the tapestry of Bernie's life, and he is a special thread that has been woven into theirs – forever.

Mattie

As an Extraordinary Minister of Holy Communion, I had been visiting homebound parishioners for quite a while. Mattie was one of the women who helped in the Sacristy after Mass each morning. She was such a bundle of joy to all of us who were with her. Eventually Mattie began to experience some memory issues. We took her absent-mindedness in stride, but then it came to the point of her not being able to be with us. Her family gave her the very best of care at home, but this formerly jovial person had now become a quiet, barely responsive person. I brought Communion to her until she was no longer able to receive, but I also provided Eucharist for her daughter and aide. On the last visit to this amazing family, I whispered a little prayer that God would give Mattie what she wished. I said good-by and went on my way, surprised that I had whispered such a prayer. Mattie passed peacefully within 30 minutes of my departure. God had heard my prayer.

Mattie was the very first person, other than family, who passed after a visit. Others followed.

Tom had been my faithful prayer partner at church for years. Together we would pray the Rosary on Saturday mornings, and he would always say we needed more people, and I would tell him we had to be patient. I can't tell how many years we prayed like that, but he was steadfast, and I was so blessed to pray with him. A fall was the beginning of his serious health problems. When he could no longer come to church, I would go visit him at home. He continued to be upbeat and fun to talk to. One Saturday I received a call from his daughter asking if would come to pray with them. Over the years I had become very close to this family, so I was more than willing to go pray with them. Together we prayed Tom's favorite prayer, the Rosary, after which I left the home. When I got back to my house, I received a call from his daughter. Tom passed peacefully 15 minutes after I left.

Both Mattie and Tom had received the Anointing of the Sick a week or two before they passed from this life. In that sacrament they were well prepared for the end of their journey in this life.

†††

Call to Rest

My child, rest in My love. Fear nothing. You are in My loving arms. No matter what problems assail you, remember always that I am with you.

Rest your head on My heart and listen to the heart songs – your heart and Mine – in unison. Let the melodies sweep you away from the noise and cares of your world. Allow yourself the joy of floating free of all your cares, all the people you nurture, and see only Me. Look into My eyes – drift into them and love yourself in Me. Float in the air of eternity and realize no one can love you with a love like Mine.

Oh Jesus, carry me away to those peaceful meadows where all is light and beauty. Let me rest there a while and be restored to wholeness, and when I leave, fill my arms with graces and blessings to bestow generously on all whom I serve in Your name.

Rest

Jesus, let me sink into You – let me not just rest my head on Your breast, but let me be lost in You so nothing remains of me but You.

Draw me into the unfathomable depths of Your love, Your life, Your very being…………..

Today, in my tiredness from all the snow clearing this week, I realized the weight of the cross (estimated at 60 lbs.)

was difficult on its own, but that cross carried the sins of the world – and You took it to Calvary with loving exhaustion to set us free. The image of the cross barely represents the reality of what You carried:

- The first sin of Adam and Eve – disobedience and pride
- The sin of Cain for murdering Abel
- The sins of the world until Noah and the cleansing waters of the flood, prefiguring Baptism
- The sins of all mankind after the flood until You came on earth.
- The sins of all the known world at the time You lived.
- The sins of men in wars and violence over these past 2000 years
- The sin of abortion and the many babies who never got to see the light of day
- The sins of their mothers and fathers
- The sins of the Holocaust and the lives of all the Jews and Catholics who died in the death camps
- The sins of all criminals from the time You walked the via Dolorosa until the time when You come again
- All the sins of the past, present and future.

My God! It's no wonder You fell so often! If we could see all our past sins and know the weight of the burden we placed on the Cross and You, truly we would repent in sack cloth and ashes. Forgive me, Jesus, for all the weight I can now set aside because You carried it in Your unbelievably great love.

†††

Ad Altare Dei

Oh Lord, You know how much I want to love You in a very deeply loving way. But what am I that You should even look in my direction? You have humbled me by calling me to Your service and exalted me at the same time. There is no way I could be deemed worthy to serve You as a Eucharistic Minister or Acolyte, but Your mercy has made it so. One thing I longed for today was that the priest or deacon would not speak so fast. They weren't really, but it might have been more meaningful if they went a little slower. Oh, if only we were able to realize deeply the greatness of the Mass, to realize intimately that You are truly present at the consecration – to see the glory of Your presence light up all the faithful people who receive You in Communion. Oh, mortal flesh which blinds the soul to the reality of the Mass! Oh Jesus, lift the veil – help us Your poor "blind" people to see the reality of You in the Eucharist!

†††

Revelation of a Reality

One weekday morning at Mass, all was as it is at every Mass. When the priest elevated the host this morning, a beautiful light emanated from It and spread across the sanctuary. When he consecrated the wine, light came up like a light beam but spilled down the sides of each of the three Communion goblets. The whole effect at first seemed to form a screen, but the Light continued to fill the whole church. At Communion time, each person was filled with this light. It was so beautiful to see the reality of the Eucharist.

†††

Leisure and Service

Have you ever felt there were just not enough hours in the day? Of that the demands being made on you were wreaking havoc with your treasured quiet time? In today's world it is easy to find ourselves struggling with the question of how much service we can give, especially if it comes at the expense of our prayer time. Can we still be good Christians if we let go of the private moments to meet the demands tugging at our proverbial "sleeves"? Many of us feel a sort of mental to leisure and service. So often we describe it as "leisure versus service."

The question perhaps is not leisure OR service but, rather, the integration of leisure AND service. Little vignettes in the Scriptures give clues to the need for both. There is one which comes readily to mind. After being at Peter's hose and curing so many people, the apostles look for Jesus the following morning. They discover him off in a "deserted" place, alone, at prayer (Mk. 1:29-39). It is not a question of choice, but a question of balance.

As a wife, mother and friend of people in towns beyond my own, I know the importance of balancing the time of doing with the time of "being." For me, it is always a question of balance. We cannot perform the day's activities well if we did not sleep well the night before. There is the day/night balance and the spring/fall, summer/winter balance. A tree cannot have branches and leaves above without roots below. Likewise, people do not function at their best unless things are balanced in their lives. The old cliché, "all work and no play makes Jack a dull boy," is quite true.

In terms of spiritual growth, a balance must be struck. One of the things I often admire, and sometimes wish I could have in my own life, is the orderliness and routine of cloistered life. Nevertheless, there is no reason why people in business or in the home cannot arrange time for leisure in the course of their day. Personally, the leisure I enjoy most takes place in the quiet early morning hours – before setting a foot on the floor. My other favorite leisure time is in the evening when, after all have gone to rest for the night, the house is

once again quiet. Christians today have no excuse for being
unbalanced when they are seeking to serve the Lord. His
kingship calls us forth into more ordered lives according to
His plan. We need to be open to this call.

In Mark 6:30-32,34, we see Jesus responding with
compassion to the crowd who "were like sheep without a
shepherd," but we must never forget that it was the Spirit that
moved Jesus in the first place. His sensitivity to the
movement of the Spirit enabled Him to perfectly fulfill the
Father's Will. A little prayer in the Sacramentary which the
priest may say before Communion reads in part: "Lord Jesus
Christ, by the WILL of the Father, and the WORK of the Holy
Spirit…" (emphasis added). This simple statement brings out
so clearly that Jesus was the perfect vessel, the pliable clay in
the Potter's hands. It is openness to the Spirit that enables us
to be more like Jesus in situations where we would rather say
NO. Above all, when we are equally willing to forego our
"programmed" leisure time, the Lord will amply provide the
rest we need at an unscheduled date. For example, a friend
once invited me to be her guest for an evening retreat
program in her parish after I had been busy with all sorts of
service-oriented activities.

The more readily we surrender to the Spirit's movement,
the better the balance between the material and spiritual
aspects of our lives. From the human point of view, things
may be very unbalanced, but overall, as seen from the
vantage point of eternity, the Lord knows where the balance

is for us. Experience is the best teacher of such truth. The more we surrender to the Lord's will in our lives the easier it is for his Spirit to influence our movements. Recognizing this through small "coincidences" is the beginning of our understanding the kind of freedom in the Spirit to which we are called. Responding to the Spirit requires setting aside periods of time for listening so we may grow in sensitivity to the Spirit's prompting or leading. As we experience the movement of the Spirit in our lives and recognize it, we are building a sure foundation that will make us quicker in our response to the Spirit. It helps us experience the reality of the phrase, "being in the right place at the right time." There is a kind of inner certainty about it. The passage from John 3:8 reminds us of how this happens: "The wind blows where it will. You hear the sound it makes but you do not know where it comes from or where it goes." In 1 Corinthians we are also given eloquent signs by which we can perceive the activity of God within ourselves: "The Spirit scrutinizes al matters, even the deep things of God." (cf. 2:10-16).

Ultimately that is the way our lives are to be lived – in total response to the Spirit. Providing leisure time, prayer time, and being open to the way the Lord wants to move in our lives is the way to achieve balance between leisure and service. Both are part of the normal Christian life. Both are necessary for us to function well as human beings. Often it feels as if we are being torn in two – being pulled in one direction or another. The tension frequently comes from our unwillingness to respond to the Spirit. We become established in a routine of prayer, leisure activity and service, and feel that anything which interrupts our schedule or throws things off is not beneficial to our spiritual growth. The opposite, however, is true. If we are so ordered in our lives as to be rigid, we are blocking the movement of the Spirit. If we accept interruptions and find peace in doing so, we can be positive the Lord is trying to rearrange our way of doing things.

Even our prayer routines can be rewritten by the Spirit. We can never expect to be like Philip (Acts 8:26-31, 39, 40), carried away by the Spirit, if we refuse to let the Spirit influence our daily activities. We must recognize the need for leisure, service, and prayer in our lives, but we must also become increasingly sensitive to the presence of the Spirit and the way the Spirit wants to influence us. It takes a lifetime of growth in this kind of sensitivity, a lifetime of listening with the heart.

Originally published by the Benedictine Convent of Perpetual Adoration, in their Spirit & Life Magazine Vol. 82:3/September-October 1986

†††

Come Watch with Me this Eventide

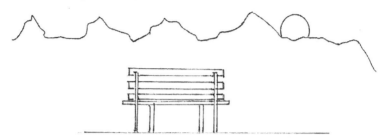

Come, watch with Me this eventide. Stand in the stillness and see.

Hear the muted songs of the birds soon to be at rest. At the time between the end of the day, when the early shades of night appear, and the last rays of sun glance across the clouds and know that at eventide all creation stands still to commune with Me. Not a breeze stirs in these special moments when the world is in transition, when the creatures of the day prepare to rest, and before the night things wake –

In this stillness I will speak to your heart. See the trees – not a leaf stirs. Now at the very top of one tree I see a few leaves stir. I know there is a gentle – very gentle – breeze. The Lord is in that breeze, but I cannot hear it. My ears become attentive and strain to hear the breeze, but it is too gentle. The noises of the world – a plane overhead, a passing car – are too loud. Silence I seek.

And yet I do hear the Lord. He speaks within my heart and calls me to look at the wispy clouds and watch as He blends the colors from grey to pink to blue and lavender.

Who could paint the vastness of the sky and change its coloring in such a variety of muted colors, but the Lord?

Come, stand with me at eventide, and be like the tree. Every single leaf – absolutely still – As the Lord touches the earth. Each branch reaches to heaven' trees are drawn forth in height and breadth, and so, the Lord would have me grow also to be reaching and stretching in all directions.

Then I notice that though the trees may lean and have branches growing in different directions, they nevertheless stand firm. Not only are they firmly rooted, but their trunks are sound. Oh Love, I thank You for this eventide. For the gift of listening to the last muted twittering of the birds settle into the hush of night. For the invitation to stand and watch You paint Your colors across the sky – just for me. For the joy of "seeing" You in that very gentle breeze that touched only a small treetop leaf, for the glory of praising You in the stillness of this eventide.

†††

Even God's Creatures...........

One morning as I stood outside the still locked doors of the church, I watched a sparrow fly with something in its beak. It landed a few feet away from me, and I could see it put a baby bird on the pavement. This action was one I'd never seen before, and the more I ponder it, the more profound its meaning becomes. I shall presume the tiny new bird was deformed in some way. The sparrow could have done any of a number of things with it like kicking it out of the nest or flying with it to a height and dropping it, but it seems even the birds of the air know Thy commandment, "Thou shalt not kill." Instead, the bird flew to the House of the Lord and lovingly abandoned this "child" to the Father's care. If it (the sparrow) had a "sense" the baby was dying, then it mercifully surrendered to God that which is God's. How simply amazing this act of merciful love on the part of the sparrow! Not a sound came from the tiny creature placed before Your earthly dwelling. How did it know to do this? What a marvelous manifestation of the perfection of Your creatures in obedience to Your decrees. They neither read nor write, yet they know their Father in Heaven. Him they serve all their days. Oh Lord! I marvel at Your wondrous deeds – Your merciful Love. If only we humans could be this attentive to You.

†††

The Riches of Silence

Silence – that most eloquent language. Silence – it punctuates our lives; every word we speak. And God dwells in that silence............in every space.....in the minute bits of nothing between our every word. Does silence scare you? Have you listened to the silence? Have you heard what it says?

Or does it make you afraid? Do you feel uncomfortable? Alone? There was once a time in my life when I could not tolerate silence............long periods of very little sound. Long periods without talking. In those time I would fill the silence with the loudness of my thoughts.

When I was in high school, we had an English teacher who taught me more about religion and God when he thought he was talking about writing and developing sensitivity to things around us. I recall quite vividly the time he asked us what we did first thing in the morning. The very first thing was to turn on the radio (or today, the television). He suggested there was a reason why we did this. I did it because the sound suggested life to me, and I did not like to be alone.

I have now found that in the silence I am not alone. The hardest thing about silence is that it is there that we meet the enemy - ourselves. In the silence we must face the cold hard facts of who we really are. Noise, sounds of any kind, represent life to most of us, yet they also camouflage reality and the source of Life. Noise is a false reality in that if we are looking for God we will most likely not find Him in noise. Elijah (1st Kings 19:9-13) heard an earthquake, a roaring fire, a mighty wind – and yet the Lord was not in these. I was struck by the next line in that passage – "and then Elijah heard the sound of a gentle breeze, and he covered his face, for the Lord God was passing." It was the sound of the breeze – not the breeze itself. Have you ever tried to listen to the sound of a gentle breeze? I did, one eventide. It was very still. It seemed to me there was no breeze at all. Yet I looked up and saw there was a breeze because a few leaves were moving at the very top of a tree. I strained my ears to hear that breeze, but I could not hear it. Then I realized how <u>still</u> Elijah had to be in order to hear that breeze. Not only physically still, but mentally still.

In my own life I have found the Lord speaks most beautifully in silence. When as a group we fall silent, I treasure it. It is in this time the Lord chooses to touch our souls. Here, our souls can speak to Him in a way that transcends thought or speech. Here is where He can most easily speak to our hearts that personal word of encouragement, support, love, tenderness, and even correction. It took an effort to move from the world so filled with noise to that place of greater quiet. It took a deliberate act of the will in this direction – an act of love. It allows our souls to rise from the hindrances we unconsciously surround it with and gives it a chance to breathe once again the clean air in which it was created and to which it longs to return. Like a prisoner set free, the soul which is set free from time to time brings back to us little tidbits of life from beyond the gray walls of our lives. Like the Dove bringing the olive branch to Noah, our souls begin to speak to us of a life far better than the life of the moment.

Silence is the precious gift of God Himself in the midst of all we do. He is present always in those trivial silences between our words, between the turning on and off of motors, in myriad other noises that fill our day. But the more space we give to the silence, the more present God can be to us.

Let us allow Our loving Father to love us in the silences of our collective prayerful gatherings. Let us listen with the ears of our hearts to His words – just for us. He loves us personally and wants to be that real to us and wants to speak to us individually. Each of us is walking a unique road to Him, so we must listen to Him for directions to stay on the right path. Silence is His gift of guidance. It is immensely rich. Let us listen to the silence and harden not our hearts, for He speaks to our hearts. Listen. Silence is more than golden..............it is the eloquent voice of God.

†††

Children....

All of you, My children, are chosen vessels. Each one has a specific mission – some visible and some hidden. Each has been given specific talents for the spread of my kingdom. Those who choose to use them rise in higher ranks through their docility and poverty of spirit, their humility, charity and patience. All of their difficulties are but stepping stones to higher sanctity. All of them lead to more intimate union with Me. Keep quiet all that you perceive because it is sacred, and all that pertains to higher realms. Each recognition with gratitude strengthens the very fiber of your soul, making you less and less susceptible to influences contrary to Mine. You are Mine, and I joy to see you aware of your sinfulness because it enables you to draw closer to Me. Be on guard, though, not to presume any constancy in My gifts. They are like little sweets I give my children to encourage them to leave more and more sin behind and stretch toward Me. All such are saints – so many hidden saints – who stand upon the ramparts defending the castle of your soul. Fear not losing your soul when you have so many cheering you on from the clouds of heaven. Truly you are Mine – now and forever.

†††

Calvary's Tomb

All was quiet in my soul – as though all is still, peaceful, and dark. There is no aridity. The thought this morning is that my soul is like the tomb in the hillside of Calvary. It quietly waits. The tomb lovingly accepts the Body of Jesus, now lifeless, spent in love for all men. It is in the tomb that the Body of Christ is sealed for a time. Let my heart, O Lord, be ready to receive you.

It is the tomb which first sees the glory of Christ emerge. IT is the tomb which sees the lifeless form of humanity not just restored but made gloriously impervious to death forever. O Lord, let us die with Thee and be sealed with Thee. In that wondrous darkness let us be transformed into Your eternal self. Let the ministering angels slowly and carefully break the seal of the tomb on Easter morning – not to let the light of the sun shine in, but to let the Light of the World shine forth from the darkness! Yes, let us die with Jesus and be transformed with Him in that quiet, peaceful, dark tomb. The tomb which gives so much is the womb of the earth. Jesus' rebirth, His transformation into the New Life, tells me I must be more than willing to die for or with Christ, but I must also be buried with Him.

Oh, blissful darkness of Calvary's tomb, the momentary resting place of our apparently fallen King. It is you, oh wondrous grave, that first knows the truth. You who first see the Light! All else is only after You have held our Savior. All else is after you first see the risen Lord. O blessed grave! It is you who held our precious Lord, though lifeless, so close to your breast, and you who also first held the Light of the World in your beautiful, sealed darkness. From you, hallowed rock, we receive the gift of new life, Glorious and Eternal.

1978

†††

Boston Marathon 2013

We learned a little while ago about the heinous explosions at the Boston Marathon. The evil within our country is increasing, and still You, our God, do not come to save us. How long, O Lord? I say with the psalmist. How long must we endure such sickening violence? How long will our enemies act with such brazenness and with impunity? They are cowards who plot against us – setting traps and running away. And You ask us to bless those who curse us – to love our enemies. So, I pray, Father forgive them, they know not what they do. But I know they know exactly what they are doing. If blessing is what You ask of us, then I need to learn more fully the power of blessings and to understand the force that comes into play through blessing. More than ever help us to put our trust in You so it can be strong and unshakeable. Mercy, Lord, for the victims and their families.

✝✝✝

Post Communion Reflection

A precious moment occurred one Thursday morning at the opening of Eucharistic Adoration. Just after the opening, I was sitting in my pew making my Thanksgiving for the great gift of Jesus in the Eucharist. It is always a unique moment in time when Jesus is both within me and before me as happened this day. This morning, though, I sensed something new. For the first time Jesus before me and within me merged into a single Presence as though He, on the altar, was one with me in my pew. There is no other way to explain it. Naturally, I would have liked to stay and literally soak in this experience. Sadly, however, I rose to attend to my after-Mass tasks, and as I did so, this beautiful experience ceased.

✝✝✝

Union

It no longer matters whether or not my physical body is ever raised from the dead. If my spirit becomes completely one with the Lord, I am then inseparably and eternally united with Him. Our physical being is, after all, only the cocoon from which one day we shall spread our wings and fly heavenward. In this life, in this body, we seek with all the directed energies and will contained herein to become more solidly united to Christ, more inflamed by His love, so utterly distracted from everything but Him, that we can spend our days loving others because we see Him in them. Oh Lord, our God, let the eyes of our souls see You in all men.

†††

In His image and Likeness

In the Mind of God, we were designed. From our limited view we can say God "imagined" how our physical forms would look. Thus, we were made in His image. Our likeness to God is our immortal soul – that likeness with God which enables us to be reunited with Him after completion of our days here on earth. God, being the Supreme Being He is, has no need of a single, physical body because He is in all things and there is nothing that is not a part of Him. Our exile on earth is a finite existence within the bounds of time, space, physical matter, and dimension. Before the fall, Adam shared the unlimited existence with God – knowing neither time nor dimension. He knew his "place" was in the Garden God gave him, and for all practical purposes it mattered not to Adam whether that Garden was Heaven or earth. He existed consciously and physically in the presence of God and simultaneously within the Heart of God. When Adam fell, he realized for the first time that he was not one with God by virtue of his physical being. He had been so one with the mind and heart of God before the fall, that his own existence as a separate entity was not known to him. It was the Tree of Knowledge of Good and Evil, the tree of Conscience, that drastically altered Adam's perspective of life.

Suddenly there was a right and a wrong where it had not existed before. The separation born of Adam's sin is that which drives us today. We all have the mind of Adam, and somewhere deep in the recesses of our minds is the certain knowledge that we have been and once again can be joyously united with Our Father Who is not only in Heaven, but also here in our hearts.

Because God is the Supreme Being Who exists everywhere, at all times, there is nothing that is not a part of Him. In the act of eating the fruit from the Tree of Knowledge of Good and Evil, Adam willfully acted contrary to the dictates of God and sadly realized that in so doing separated himself from God. During his intimate union with God, Adam knew only the love, and peace and goodness of the Father. By his act of disobedience, Adam became sorrowfully aware of sin and the pain of separation. The great goodness and beauty of which he once was a part were lost, but the knowledge, the memory of that glory remained in Adam's mind. It is still with us today.

†††

Faith and Hope

What more beautiful sign of hope can You give us, Lord, than snowdrops in bud, springing forth from the frozen ground, amidst snow and ice? Your power, O Lord, to bring life from the most frozen of ground can only serve to remind us that no matter how cold and unmoving we may be, no matter how much ice there may be upon our brow, no matter how cold our stony hearts may be, Your life in us cannot be inhibited in the same way the frozen ground does not prevent the snowdrop from making its way, through Your remarkable and mysterious power, to the surface – even though the ground may be immovable in all other ways. Once it reaches the light of the sunshine, it is made soft and tender and responds to the gentlest of breezes, despite the fact that the tender blossom is surrounded by snow and ice. Its rising through the snow draws the warmth of the sun into itself, and as it becomes warmed, the ice slowly melts away in a circle all around.

So, too, the gifts of faith and hope in us are like this flower which struggles to blossom amidst all adversity. It is in darkness and despair that we learn we have faith and hope. Even in darkness we feel ourselves drawn to reach out into that which we cannot see and do not know. But we reach – for our darkness and despair are so bleak that to reach is infinitely better than to remain where we are. We struggle, an as we near the surface, we sense an increasing warmth and that encourages us even further. Then, we lease expect, we break forth into the glorious light of Christ. This little, tiny "thing" in us has made it to the surface, and we rejoice greatly, but we do not stop there. We continue to reach out, seeking to come more closely united with our Light. As we stretch, we become like a small green shoot that mysteriously forms a bud. As time passes, the glory of the Lord is made manifest as that "bud" is transformed into a beautiful tender flower in full bloom which nods ever so gently in the breezes of the Holy Spirit, and it smiles because now it sees that the cold ice and snow which surrounded it have been melted away all because we dared to struggle to reach up and touch the Light of the world!

1978

†††

Have you seen Christ lately?

I saw Him the other day in the supermarket, an old man slightly confused at the various prices of things, and people were ignoring him – no one stopped to ask how he was doing.

I saw Him at the checkout register – a little old lady who was having a hard time putting her 13 items on the counter of the 12-item express line. I saw the scowl of the clerk at the extra item, and the irritation of those behind her because of her slowness. I saw Him along the highway. His car had broken down, and no one stopped to help.

He was in the nursing home, sitting in a wheelchair, staring out a window. His face was sad. It seemed to me He was wondering if anyone would remember He was there. At the high school I saw Him. He was the frail student whose shy ways and quiet manner made Him the butt of so many foolish jokes and cruel teasing.

I saw him on the playground, the young child being taunted by the older children. I heard His pleas to have His toy returned, but it fell on deaf ears." I saw Him walking downtown – a solitary figure, slightly bent and using a cane. No one smiled at Him.

I saw Him in the crippled people who were trying to live life the best way they could, despite their handicaps, and I saw the way people looked at them. Their faces spoke one word – ignore.

Then I saw Him as a newcomer to town and noticed how little people did to make Him feel welcome. He stood in the midst of those who profess to be His followers, but they did not see Him.

Oh, Lord, how often have I seen You this day? How often have I passed by when I should have slowed my pace and recognized You? Weren't You the old man driving his car at 35 miles per hour in the 40 mph zone? Couldn't I have been a bit more patient and understanding? Weren't you the confused person at the intersection at whom passing motorists shouted obscenities? Oh, Lord! Forgive me my blindness and help me see You more clearly in all I meet.

1979

†††

Weeds and Sin

Sometimes the most ordinary of activities can lead to a deeper reflection on an important subject. Most people understand sin as a basic disobedience to God. How it anchors itself in the soul is not even considered. Today, though, I was doing the simple task of pulling weeds – not from a flower bed, but from the lawn itself. How did so many of them get there?

The answer to that was pretty obvious – my neighbor has a yard full of these weeds, and the north wind doth blow them in my direction. They are a curious weed because when they blossom, they can be very pretty. In the wild and untamed we are mesmerized by the beauty of this sudden patch of color amidst the usual greens of summer. However, almost as a hands-on contrast of the parable of the weeds and the wheat, these weeds have a particularly nasty habit of living in the shady places of the lawn, so they are not easily seen. Once one of them gets anchored in the soil, numerous tentacles spread out in all directions, frequently crossing over each other and putting down further roots. They come up in the grassy areas and eventually form a solid mass that blocks out the grass completely.

This afternoon I started to pull up a small patch of these weeds. Then I noticed another small patch not too far away, and yet another, and another. Sin is very much like these weeds. When it begins to take root in the soul, it seems so small and insignificant. Contrast that with venial sin. It seems harmless enough. If left untended, this innocuous weed slowly but deftly takes root within us. The movement of this one sin (it doesn't matter what kind of sin it is), happens when we are not looking. Then one day we will look at our souls and see this tangled web of evil and wonder how it got there.

All of the spiritual masters warn us about the effects of sin, but this weed in the lawn is an up close and personal look at what it does. Eventually we decide we need to get rid of this weed (sin) and try to rip it out. The lawn looks good, but we did not get all the roots, so the weed will come back. It's not easy to eradicate something once it gets established. For many of us this is a life-long battle. Of course, we can go buy weed killer and feel we have been successful, but we tend to forget that the winds carry these weeds to our lawn (and sin gets carried into our souls through things like television, movies, and questionable company). While some people may think it foolish to make frequent confessions (at least once a month), it is this very action which helps eradicate those pesky habits or failures which will eventually lead us away from the God Who loves us so much. Of how much greater value is our own soul than a lawn of green grass? When we are judged, will it be on how weed-less our lawn was or on the beauty of our souls? Take a look at the weeds around you. The "weeds" in your soul are far more dangerous than the ones in the lawn, but look at the lawn anyhow to get an idea of how many weeds there are and then reflect on what your soul looks like. Which would you rather have – a weed-free lawn or a sin-free soul?

†††

The Flower Garden

This spring I planted a garden. How lovely it would be, marigolds and Impatiens, asters for later, you see. The plants were all set then, neatly in a row. They all looked so pretty, with lots of room for them to grow. And so my lovely garden was arranged in the spring. Fluffy soil and tender plants needing not a thing. Later a few weeds appeared. They seemed as not a threat, and so to thoughts of weeding, I merely said, "not yet."

The summer found me busy, running here and there. My once lovely garden looked as though I didn't care. Finally, one August eve I looked and was dismayed. My once lovely flowers stood in the tall weeds' shade. So bending down, I took a clump of weeds in my hand and found beneath the tall weeds, close to the moist earth, other leaves were rotting, going to their new birth. A persistent pink petunia stood high among the weeds - a gift to me from the Lord, for I'd not planted any seeds. And as I yanked and pulled the unwanted ones away, I looked and found I'd pulled the petunia to my great dismay. Leaving the weeds to the harvest, I soon began to recall, was the Lord's command. Perhaps I should have left them to the fall.

For as I tore the unwanted flowers, as weeds so oft turn out to be, I discovered other things of great value to me. Though weeds may come and over grow a garden so it isn't neat, still all the flowers were there – every one was at my feet.

The weeds that came had shallow roots, tap root and side root, none of them deep. So, I also discovered how the good of the earth are all still there – and they're not asleep. Though ugliness would upset my garden bed, still my lovely plants, through the tall weeds shade, were all moisture-fed. So we, who follow the Lord, are like the lovely flowers with evil all around, but fed by the Spring showers, seemingly over-powered, yet rooted in His Love. Which is why He says we must struggle and wait until the harvest for weeds are the first of all the plants to die, and then we, the flowers, will hold our heads - Up high!

1978

†††

The Mockingbird

Consider the gift of the mockingbird. It has no song of its own, but it takes the songs of all the other birds and orchestrates them into the most glorious symphony of song. No other bird has the ability to change its sound and master such a wonderful combination of songs. While all the other birds are limited to the song they must sing, our brother mockingbird, in simple brown garb, takes the song of each and composes a medley. In this one little bird is a wealth of song. In this one little bird is a multitude of gifts; where else or how else, except for the mockingbird, can we sit and listen to the songs of so many birds from the throat of just one! What joy! What a remarkable gift the Lord has given to this little bird, and even more remarkable that in singing its praises to the Lord of All Creation, our hearts can be stirred, our ears attuned, and joy reign supreme within us. For in giving the gift to this dull colored bird, the Lord, has given us a gift also. Let us never forget that outward appearance is not of supreme importance; it is the appearance within, the use of the gifts contained therein. And such royal gifts do we as people have from the hands of Jesus. If we cannot take the time to glory in the gifts given to a simple little bird, how much less can we appreciate the gifts of God to us which are of much greater value.

When we learn to appreciate and value greatly the simplest things of life, we begin to appreciate even more the gifts of greater value from our Creator. For without the gift of hearing, we would not hear the song of the mockingbird. Without the gift of sight, we could not be thankful for its dull color which protects it and so ensures that we might be privileged to hear its song. Now in the spring, we are also so very thankful for the gift of smell – to know that a hyacinth is in bloom, or a lilac. Or to smell grass that is cut for the first time this season. Oh, how glorious are the gifts of the Lord to us! Let us always proclaim His greatness and thank Him for making us the way He made us. To touch the petal of a tulip, shiny and soft and so silky..........to see beds of flowers in bloom.........to smell the fragrance of the earth which ascends like a sweet perfume before the Throne of God. How blessed we are that we can share in these things which God made.

In this time of rebirth and renewal of the earth, let us glory in the wonders of the Lord – the way the trees send forth their own very special pale yellow-green clusters of blossoms, and the way the world takes on the delicate color of new life. Let us never forget to be sensitive to these wonders around us. In being thrilled by all these things we can ever so much more appreciate how wonderful is the world made for us by our Creator! Al glory and honor and praise to our Mighty God, for His works ae truly marvelous to behold!

†††

Confession

Lord, I am a sinner who talks too much. I must be on my guard lest sharing become gossiping. There is a fine line. Help me to maintain the silence which must, of necessity, be maintained because of the trust people have shown me. Oh, God, I feel like a bumbling idiot! I feel as though I'm a glory-seeker who's reaping her just rewards of praise and boasting of Your wonders here and now, and that when I am finally called to You it will be only to hear that I've received the reward of my labors! See what a foolish child I am! Oh Lord, God, have pity on me!

How long it has been since I sat in silence. Too many are the thoughts that through my head fly. Too many the things commanding my attention. My God, where are You? I cry. I feel as though I'm stumbling along a darkened way. My prayer time seems to be crumbling - Oh, Lord! Let me not stray! You know my heart belongs to You. Take my time, every moment too. Take my mind, my hands, my ears; Integrate them with your life in me now and for all my years. This is a vale of tears, a very tough road to "hoe." But Lord, if You'll be with me, I'll make it, I just know.

†††

The Joys of Heaven

God's unending presence * The company of countless saints * The reunion with family members back to the beginning * The beauty of paradise * The joy of good health, never growing tired, never being hungry, never having to watch our weight or blood pressure, never being sick again or needing protection from diseases * No financial worries or cares about a roof over our head, * No taxes to pay, * No shopping or laundry to be done, * No maintenance concerns for house, car, or ourselves. * Instead, we will be focused on the sound of God's voice, or that of Jesus or Mary, watching over our families and interceding for them * Being completely at peace.

†††

My Little Candle

"Tonight, my heart sings." My life, like a candle, burns, My Lord, for Thee' let my life, like a candle burn only just for Thee.

Let my life burn like a candle down to the smallest flame, and while there is light, let it praise Your Name. Let my life burn like a candle through the night, and let it end its night long vigil with the dawn of Heaven's light.

Let my life burn like a candle for all those in need let it bring them peace and comfort and know that You heed. Tiny prayers barely spoken, from hearts greatly broken, from words that can't be said, knowing they were spoken when dying, You bled. Oh, my Jesus, what can I tell You Who know our thoughts so well? Fill our hearts with Your love, Lord So that others for You may swell. Oh, my Jesus, my Lord, my Savior, my God, my all may I always prostrate before You fall. In the keeping of Your hearing let us not worldly sing, for only You, my love, are my King.

✝✝✝

Fire and a Cold Night

One cold, moonless winter night when there was a good fire roaring in the fireplace, I decided just to sit quietly for a while. The house was still. As I sat, relaxed, but tired, I drifted and became aware of how we always are attracted by the brilliance and liveliness of flames dancing on logs, but this night the thought occurred to me that the flames were representative of how we often think of God's love – something quite visible and eye-catching. As I pondered this further, I decided that is how God's love first comes to us – with much life, heat, and color. We seem to want His love to be like that always, but then I realized in the fire that the flames were only a "surface" activity – that the real transforming of the log to ashes came from the hot embers they became after the flames disappeared. So, God's love in us must become more like the hot embers, not a splash of color and attractiveness on the outside, but the real "heat" of the embers which contain the transforming power of our Eternal Father. Our very lives are changed interiorly when the igniting flames do not go out but become the concentrated heat of love and dedication that burns so fiercely within us as to transform us – thus making it possible for Christ to become more and more visible in the world through our lives. The joy of being a burning ember is the joy of being consumed in and by the love of God.

1979

†††

What is Man.....

What is man that You should keep him in mind, Lord? You have made him a little less than the angels. Yet, when I see my planet with Your "eyes" (the Hubble telescope) and can see the grandeur of the universe, I know two things: the greatness of Your Majesty and Infinite Beauty and my own nothingness. I am greatly humbled when I realize the Lord of All Creation loved, and loves, us so much as to lay aside His greatness, His Glory, His Power, and reduce Himself to become one like us – in all things, except sin. That His love for us, His little creatures, impels Him to reach not down, but out to us in human form. That He would let us see Him face to Face and call us to Himself. That, being totally Complete in the Trinity, He nevertheless desires the love of the work of His hands.

Oh, foolish children are we who do not even try to reach out to the One Who is Perfect Love. He Who has given us the ability to see distant galaxies and nebulae also gives us even more reason to acknowledge His existence and praise Him for all the heavenly glory with which He is surrounded. How dare we ignore His infinite designs? He Who placed our little planet amidst so many great lights deserves our thanks and adoration. He has placed us on a planet that floats unsuspended in space. That thought alone is enough to take your breath away.

Why then, if we know this, do we not take better care and love each other? It's more than just taking care of "Mother Earth." It's about respect for each other aware that the Power which created the enormity of the universe and which lives within each of us. Each person is Awesome – not because of how they look – but because they carry within them the Spirit of the same Living God who creates constantly and has let us see some of His glories in the universe.

Oh Lord, Our Creator and Ultimate Goal, draw us to an awareness of how great the dignity of each person is because Your Presence in us gives life.

†††

The Love of the Women of His Day for Jesus

During His life on earth, Jesus was never romantically linked with any woman. His relationship with Mary was special, but She is His Mother. If Jesus had at any point taken a woman into His arms during His stay in the same manner as most men, His life and all that He did would have been open to scandal and ridicule. His celibacy set Him apart, yet women were still attracted to Him. What was His charisma that so charmed women to travel at the edges of His circle? Why was it always the women who cared for His physical needs?

Historically women of Jesus' time were the quiet, hard-working partners of a team headed by their husbands. There had to be something more to Jesus that would make these women leave their homes, voluntarily, and serve Him. What was it?

For one thing, Jesus exuded gentleness – He, a grown Man of 30 or so years – just *looked* gentle. He *looked* gentle. He *looked* touchable. In the Divine Plan God so created woman that she cannot resist gentleness and tenderness. There isn't a newborn baby that doesn't have it. Perhaps another word is innocence. And so even though Jesus was now fully grown, the women around Him recognized these "fragilities" in Our Lord and responded by maternal instinct.

There was something else the women saw in Jesus – it was compassion. In those days, the men did their work and the women consoled each other at the well or when they did their washing. With Jesus there was a unique, semi-intuitive way of communicating with the ladies. His smile, the light in His eyes communicated that He felt, He knew, He understood the female mind. No other man had come along who was so very open and approachable. Without a word, He welcomed them. Without a touch, He kissed them. With only His eyes, He melted their hearts. And with all their natural loving womanly ways, they sought to do things for Him as a sign of their reaction to Him………..as a gentle, unaffected, unobtrusive way of displaying their great adoration for Him.

A simple thing – but for the women who knew Him then, it must have been quite powerful – to find in their midst a Man who truly knew and understood the female mind.

1977

†††

What is in a Name?

There once was a woman who in her life had been known by many different names. As a child she was called by the name given her by her parents. As she grew up, she was called by the nickname her friends gave her. Then she married and was called by yet another name. Two or three times she was widowed and remarried, and thus she had still other names. And when she served in the military, she was addressed by yet another name. Finally, the woman died, and God asked her name. When she replied, He asked her about the other names she had during her life. And truthfully, she answered. You are true in your statements, said the Lord, but by what name were you called the day you were born? And thinking a moment, the woman answered that she was born without a name, and the first gift she received was her name from her parents. What other gifts did you receive from the first, asked the Almighty. Then she replied that first of all she had received the gift of life from Him. Delighted with her simple and forthright reply, the Lord asked her what things she did for Him in her life. Lord, she answered, there was nothing that I did for You during my life. And at this she hung her head. But the Lord reached out to her and lifted her chin. Why do you say you did nothing for Me? He asked. For in all you did in your life for others, you have done as much for Me. And now finally you are welcome here, but all the gifts you received from your parents are not recognized here, and neither is the name they gave you. But, Lord, she answered, by what name then shall I be called? To all here, He replied, you shall be known as My Daughter.

1977

†††

The House of the Lord

This is the House of the Lord, This is My Dwelling Place. Sweep clean the dust from the corners – light a lamp, and keep it lit in anticipation of My coming.

†††

Gifts

If we were to tally all the gifts and favors You have given us, Oh Lord, there would not be enough paper in the world to do so.

Every breath we take is a gift from You; every movement we make is a gift from You. Would that we could become sensitive enough to all the mercies of Your generous Heart.

†††

Road to Sinai

The artist picked up a brush, and, without any precon-
ceived idea, began to apply paint to the empty canvas. Colors
appeared, some reminiscent of a desert, others of distant
hills, and a blue sky with windswept clouds at the top. As the
artist looked, a trail wound its way through the sand and
seemed to disappear at the base of the mountains. The two
mountain peaks were like guardians on either side of the
barely discernable trail. The artist put the brushes down and
stared at the image. After a difficult day recently, the artist
wondered why the desert was so inviting. Perhaps it was the
absence of people and words. However, the desert is also a
place of spiritual combat.........making it a less inviting
place. But the Desert Fathers and Mothers sought such a
place in which to live. The solitude combined with the stark
beauty of the desolate place became their home because they
would spend their days and nights in prayer, seeking God. It
is from this very desolate place we have inherited the wisdom
of the Desert Fathers and Mothers. The readings of the
Desert Fathers and Mothers shows the result of such spiritual
combat. Like anything in this life, without exercise and effort,
our spirits would grow weak. We need those gale winds and
storms to grow in the confidence that assures us that with
You, our God, there is absolutely nothing to fear.

Music

There is no beautiful classical music being created in these days because man has chosen to surround himself with dissonance and disharmony. He is at war with nature. All the great music came from people who dearly loved nature and wrote their music to the glory and honor of God. They who serve their God first shall reap the echoes of the Hosannas in Heaven in their music for He shall have a perfectly joyful noise made unto Himself.

Alleluia!

††††

Adoration Day

Before Your Eucharistic Face, Lord, I sit, reflecting on Your many graces and the people who have been helped by my words. Today I pray that You will continue to give me graces not for myself, but for others, the souls You will send me...

††††

This morning there was a phone call, which lasted quite some time, from a searching soul who turned to me because she felt "drawn to me" as she said. Lord, You alone know what transpired and how, later, once again I was exhausted and needed to rest.

"You can be a vessel only as long as you are docile to My Will. I have chosen that it be so. Leave all other concerns behind. Keep the eyes and ears of your heart attuned to My Spirit within you. As the wind blows, so shall you be – as my hands, as a reflection of My love to others, as a source of comfort – whatever I need you to bring to those whom I send you. You are no longer your own – you are mine – and I have need of you to bring My love to others. You already know the joy which comes of obedience and ministry."

†††

On Another Adoration Day

Coming to Silence

To hear God speak we need to become silent, not just be in a silent, quiet place. How often it happens that when we come into a church to sit in adoration of the Eucharistic Lord that many thoughts start to run through our heads. The events of the day, the chores waiting for us when we get home, any of a number of things which need to be done before sleeping. The list can get very long. Trying to quiet our very active mind can seem like an exercise in futility from time to time. One of the first things that helps is to just sit, relax, and take a few deep breaths. Then imagine you are in a beautiful place. Let this place become clear in your mind and imagine not only that you are there, but that Jesus Himself is there with you. For some people reading a guided reflection or meditation helps transition from the world "out there" to the quiet of the world within yourself. Using any number of spiritual books also helps to readjust our minds. It takes some practice to let go of all the daily activities and just sit quietly. Imagery of Christ, His apostles, and others from Scripture helps us sink more deeply into that inner world of the spirit. It takes time and effort to make this change from the outside world to the inner world of the Spirit, and when it does begin to happen, you may find yourself quietly aware of peaceful thoughts and remembrances of graces given and sense a spirit of gratitude. Everyone comes to this inner stillness in their own unique way, but everyone can reach this pool of inner calm. It is here where we can deeply encounter God and "hear" His Voice. Be at peace......all is well. Listen to Him.

In each soul I work differently. No two are alike – like the snowflakes. Each has a unique charism or mission. Each is called to purification in order to grow in virtue. The long journey begins here on earth and does not end. In heaven the gifts received and used at the prompting of my Spirit are transformed because the soul is then abiding in Me always and will never again sin or stumble. Their journey brings them into complete union with Me. Therefore, they are like unto Me and rejoice to follow My commands. There is no doubt about what I ask. There is no hesitation in responding to any request. All is done in joy for all in heaven are in complete union with My spirit. Growth on earth is preparation for the work of heaven, and there is never a lack of work, no drudgery, no tiredness in My presence.

Eternity is a state of everlasting bliss – in My presence and in the company of all the souls who were diligent in their pursuit of Me. However, it was diligence in response to My call to them to seek and find Me.

Listen and attend to those subtle stirrings in the secret places of your heart and mind. Do not doubt, but act in faith and you will see even more wondrous moments than those you have already seen. I truly am your Lord and God. Each surrender draws you closer to My heart. Each surrender is a victory, not defeat as the world would call it. Trust ever more and more. Do not be afraid of failing. Even "failure" is a blessing when it brings forth growth & change for a closer walk with Me. Never fear, be always at peace and be assured that peace is the gift I give you. Repeat your fiat often and with confidence. You are Mine and I love you with an eternal love.

††††

Dust and Ashes

Except for Ash Wednesday, how often do we remind ourselves of the brevity of our journey here on earth? This afternoon I had a stark reminder of the shortness of life. An innocent little sparrow flew into the back door of the porch. It fell to the deck and breathed only briefly and then was very still. It broke my heart. This innocent, sweet little songbird will sing no more. Oh, how I prayed it would breathe again – and fly again – and sing once more. I hoped in vain. It was still warm when I picked it up and gently cradled it in a paper towel. Oh, the details in this tiny bird's makeup! The colors in the feathers, the incredibly small feet and the claws that were surprising in length. Its tail feathers were on the long side, considering the smallness of this bird. As I let it sit, wrapped safely in the paper towel, I needed to decide what to do next. Easily I could have just dumped it in a waste pail, but that did not seem right. And then I remembered: "You are dust and to dust you will return." So, this little creature, formed by the love of God, was given a place to rest, buried under a pile of decaying vegetation in a place not likely to be disturbed. Somehow, that seemed to be the right thing to do – to render unto God the things that are God's.

2020

✝✝✝

Night Watch

Tonight, I saw again my favorite star – a bright, stunning planet that I have watched since it rose. Like the most brilliant of diamonds, it is absolutely sparkling, scintillating, in the night sky. I claim it as my star – although nothing is really mine. But when I see it, it is like falling in love. It is Your creation, Lord. In my heart I kneel before You, grateful for this evening star. If we could thank You for all the beauty in the world, we still would fall so very, very short of the praise we owe You for everything else You've created just so we could live on this planet. How marvelous then must heaven be.

†††

The Creator

You, God, we call Creator. You love to create, and love is the energy which causes such beauty to burst forth. We see it here on this planet in the diversity of landscapes, flowers, animals, fish, and birds. How can man look at these things and not praise You for all this?

†††

Advent

How quickly we forget that Advent, similar to Lent, is not just a time of preparation – it can also be a time of trial. St. Faustina is an extreme example, but from her we see that the closer a soul approaches perfection, the more they become tested by the evil one – only to struggle through and rely on God all the more, thereby becoming a stronger soul, more confident in You, our God. St. Pio of Pietrelcina is another example. Both of these saints had mystical experiences from a young age, but despite their closeness to God they show us how to combat the inevitable assaults as we reach out to You, our God. Let us invoke their help as we prepare for the Birth of Christ.

††

The Nativity

Christmas Day – A few days ago as I reflected on the poverty of the stable where Jesus was born, I thought of recent comments that the stable was a smelly place because of the animals. Then it occurred to me the stable was the perfect place for the Newborn Babe. It was a place without sin. Any man-made shelter for Him, like an inn, would have been a sin-filled place in many ways, both great and small. Where else should we find our Creator except among the domestic creatures He made: sheep, cattle, donkeys, and maybe a couple of chickens or ducks. These animals would not only welcome their Lord and Master, they would also bow before Him and keep Him warm on a cold winter night. The animals did what humans refused to do. They responded to His Presence with perfect obedience!

Oh, how foolish we are, Lord, to look and not see, to hear and not comprehend. Knowing how of old You provided for the Israelites – water from a rock, bread from heaven, etc., - how is it we are surprised Your first "home" is a stable? These many years later, it makes perfect sense.

†††

Christmas Present – A few days after Christmas, in the early hours before the church opened, a lone figure approached the Nativity scene which was in front of the altar. The person knelt in prayer. Then, the person gently picked up the infant Jesus and held Him close. In the silence of the church a beautiful lullaby could be heard. The sound was truly angelic. It went on for some time - just the most beautiful melody one had ever heard, lifting the spirit and soul toward the heavens. The person was singing to Jesus. A sense of awe came over me – and reverence as well. I could have stayed there all day, but after several minutes the Baby Jesus was gently returned to his place and the person left. Was it one of the heralding angels?

†††

The Boat

I am a small boat adrift on an immense sea. I have no recollection of how I got here, nor do I know where I am going. My boat and I must have gone through a dreadful, terrible storm and now my boat has no rudder. I drift and my talents drift – all the while missing the rudder on my little boat so I might one day find my way home.

†††

A Reflection on the Soul and Singing

As consciousness slowly returns, my mind is aware of Alleluias being sung in my heart. Be still, my mind, and listen to the joyous song. My mind is curious, so I turn on the light. It is 4 a.m. I turn off the light and enthralled, listen to the silent Alleluias rising from my heart. Do not cease your song, my soul! Some minutes later the alarm rings, again, and it is time to rise – but oh, how could one move from this spot and disturb the Alleluias? Nevertheless, my body must rise, and the Alleluias, like a flock of angels, slowly fade, leaving my heart aching for their company.

†††

God gives His people many different gifts. Psalm 127 tells us that "He pours gifts on His beloved while they slumber." Sometimes we can be surprised by the gifts God gives us even when we are sleeping. For instance, there was a case when a person woke up with an awareness of music literally in their soul. It was so beautiful the person did not move, but instead focused on this awareness of music that sounded so familiar to them. In the early morning silence, they recognized the melody as an old Eucharistic hymn. They finally realized the hymn was "Jesus, my Lord, my God, my All." For quite some time they were attuned to this melody within them. Finally, they arose and looked through their music. They found the hymn, but quickly realized the melody they had "heard" was not what was in the old hymnal. It was different. Enchanted, they figured out what the notes were on the piano. It was a puzzlement. Eventually they came across some literature which addressed the question – does the soul sing? Yes, the soul "sings" when we use our intellectual powers of the soul through our vocal chords. The problem with the answer is that the vocal chords were silent, and the music was heard in a different manner, which could not be explained. Apparently this unusual "gift" of God is something several people have experienced. Because of its hard to explain nature, people do not talk about it, but it is quite possible that if we "hear" within us beautiful heavenly music, then we can relax and be thankful because it is truly a gift from God.

We can relate this kind of experience to the Gospel story of the Pearl of great price – the hidden treasure in the field, or the incredible pearl. Bishop Robert Barron in an essay for the 19th Sunday in Ordinary Time, several years ago, wrote "...when the inexhaustible desire (of your spirit) is fitted to the inexhaustible God, then the heart sings – for it has found "what no thief or moth can destroy."

A concluding Prayer for the above reflection

It is not enough for us to begin to learn these things about the "pearl of great price" which is our soul. Reawaken us, Lord, to the beautiful reality of Your Presence in our soul. Help us understand that to surrender to Your Divine Will in our lives is to step onto the road to joy and freedom that only You can give. Help us, Lord, we pray, to make reparation for our own ignorance and failures for so long. Teach us Your ways, Oh Lord, and we will rejoice to do Your Will. Amen.

†††

A letter to a friend

It was 4 a.m., and in my mind was this letter to a friend. I found words echoing those effusive passages in Scripture, some of Paul's letters to the early Christians. An experience of love swelled with my heart, crying out to be given away, and being extremely humbled at its intensity because this was not human love – it was a tiny inkling of God's great love for us, it brought tears to my eyes. "Love isn't love until it is given away," (I wrote). The phrase is truer than many understand. Recognizing how profound the experience was, I told my friend that now we can understand why Jesus and Mary practically cry out to us in tears. The love of God is so great and is there for us, but we stupid and foolish humans are satisfied to sit in the mud when, if we turned to God, we would experience such love and joy that defies words and come to understand in a little way why God "cries" when we refuse His great and merciful love. Oh, that our hearts would open wide to receive His love! The whole world would be so totally beautiful, and perhaps all the plants and animals would reveal so much more to us if we were filled with this love, because even they would detect it.

†††

All Souls Day

At Mass one All Souls Day our Deacon spoke of how at this time of the year the souls of the dead can come to request our prayers. Never hearing of this before, it sounded strange. But that year I had a dream of my maternal grandfather, and he brought a relative with him whom I did not know, and for whom I was to pray. The Deacon's homily made a lasting impression. It also inspired me to be more prayerful for our deceased family members and others we have known and who have gone to their eternal reward. It is always a surprise how God works in our lives, and praying for our loved ones is something we must not forget, for one day we will wish that there were people praying for us after we have been called from this life.

Night Prayers

The day is ending. Shadows lengthen as the sun sinks slowly into the west. Evening prayers rise softly, and heavy eyelids close as slumber overtakes a tired body. Prayers begun silently drift heavenward, fading into the night. At midnight, an angel's wing softly brushes the face of the sleeping soul. Effortlessly the soul rises in the darkness and continues the prayers left unfinished. In peace it gently slips back into rest to await the dawn.

CRIES TO GOD

When a soul is in anguish, it cries to God, by accident or design. There is no other direction for the soul to face, except upward to the Eternal Heavens and the God Who dwells there.

†††

April 16 – My Lord & My God – We feel like the psalmist who cries out "how long, oh Lord?" We have neither prophet nor priest to tell us when this will end. Therefore, Oh Lord, we beg You for the peace of heart and patient endurance to survive these unusual circumstances. Have mercy on families with small children who cannot comprehend what is going on and why they cannot do some things.

†††

April 18 – My Jesus, tonight we cry tears within our hearts. We so miss the consolation, the peace in our hearts, with which we began this odyssey – and which still continues until a time which only You know. We miss the joy of ministry, the routine of our former spiritual life. Oh Lord our souls are like a dry, parched land longing for a gentle rain. It is like a nomad crossing the trackless wastes of the desert.

The night comes and we are so tired we cannot lift our eyes to the stars and gaze on the wonders Your hands have made. They do not inspire us now. Our souls are dumb, silent, and still.

†††

Lord, tonight I am exhausted. I care not what the morrow brings – only that it brings me You. You are all I long for tonight. The façade of the strong, independent woman is gone. All that is left is the girl whose strength you were. Please, my Love, don't let the enemy overpower me or subdue me. I need Your strength – I need You beside me so I can be strong, but most of all, I need Your Love.

†††

April 24 – Lord, for the great blessing of Your protection through the intercession of our Blessed Lady, we are most grateful. May Your protective hand be upon us through this time of trial, and when it ends, may we be found steadfast and faithful. For all the graces and blessings of this day, we humbly thank You.

†††

April 26 – Oh Lord, our souls are now like a lifeless desert. Nothing moves or grows there. It has become a kind of spiritual wasteland. However, we are determined to be steadfast through this trial. All we ask is Your love and peace in our hearts.

††††

April 30 – Lord, more than anything else we long for the grace to remain strong in the faith, loving and compassionate to all we serve, and silent in the face of people who think (or seem to think) of no one other than themselves, thereby causing hardship for others. Keep is focused in prayer and always attuned to Your Voice.

†††

Notice was received that we would soon re-open the church for public Mass.

May 1 – Oh Jesus, we look forward to going to church and receiving You in the Eucharist. All these days have been more like being in a desert, needing to forage for sustenance. Oh Lord, You have been so good to us. We feel spiritually faint from lack of Your provision for us because of the pandemic. There are no aides to come to our help, so we struggle through each day – disorganized and feeling disoriented. Jesus, we need Your help else our small boat will be lost in a strange sea.

†††

May 3 – Oh Lord. You know I care very deeply for people. There is in me a tremendous compassion for the ill. These days I am not able to visit this family or others. Your servant has been relieved of her service. It is a strange thing. I am most grateful to our pastor that he asked me to continue to open the church in the morning. It is a gift to do so, and it gives me quiet time with You.

†††

May 12 – Day 57 without Mass. – My Lord, there is something special in what feels like grace in the meeting this evening with Ramah, the UPS driver who parked his truck in front of my house. My dog was acting like he wanted to go outside, so we went out, and that is when I saw the truck. My friendly dog wanted to say hello to the driver, and so we met. The driver had a box of dog biscuits with him, and I told him how much I enjoyed the UPS video of the drivers and the animals they meet along the route. It turned out that he knows Tim the UPS driver who used to deliver merchandise to us when we had a retail store. Ramah told me how long his day is and that he had no helper. I told him I would pray for him, and he promised to tell Tim I said hello. It was such a touching encounter. So, Lord, I place Ramah in Your heart and mine that he be protected from illness. Please keep him and all UPS drivers healthy and safe.

†††

May 19 – 64th day without Mass. – Oh Jesus, as we count the number of days without a public Mass, we are reminded of the Israelites and their 40-year journey from Egypt to the Promised Land. It makes our difficulties pale in comparison. Certainly, we pray this global health issue will not last that long. The people of today would not survive that long a "journey." People have no excuses during this trial. Many people have chosen to live without You, my God. They have become progressively worse in their lack of adherence to the 10 Commandments. How can they possibly expect You to generously bless them when they persist in denying You exist? Self-discipline comes from loving You and obeying the commandments You gave us. Oh Lord, how kind and merciful You are to put up with us one day at a time. As for Your children, we choose to follow You despite our weak faith.

"As for me and my house, we will follow the Lord."

†††

June 1 – Oh Lord, have mercy on all Your children and bring us safely through this time of trial. Bring peace to Minneapolis where a police officer killed a man, and then riots and looting followed. Civilized people do not act like animals. The outburst of anger was uncontrolled and one suffering led to more innocent people suffering. What has happened to this world? I know – they have forgotten You, the Prince of Peace.

†††

June 5 – My Lord, despite the strangeness of our world for these months, You have sustained us. We are so grateful that some of us have a little ministry in the morning with time in Your presence and the silence of the church. You have blessed us with peace and perseverance, for which we are most grateful, but we am also grateful for the graces, blessings, and Your protection during these very trying days.

†††

June 8 – Weekday Mass Resumes – Oh Lord, how wonderful it was to be back in our church, even if we were wearing masks. To hear our pastor celebrate the Eucharist was like coming alive once more. Receiving the Eucharist was like water on the tongue of a person who has crossed a large, barren desert. And then, we left the church. Yes, it was strange, but it was also a big sign of hope. Better yet, we were together with You at last!

†††

July 4th – Our First Weekend Mass – Gratitude. What a privilege it was to be at the first weekend Mass in all these months. Oh Lord, we thank you from the bottom of our hearts, from the depths of our souls, that we could once again be in Your House. At this Mass, the most "joyful noise" was the sound of human voices responding to the prayers or saying them together. The empty echo was gone, and while it was not exactly as things were when we were silenced, at least we had the main parts of the Mass and a sense of community reunited. The most difficult part, beginning with our weekday Masses, is that we can receive Eucharist but must leave the church immediately after that. We did not have the comfort of sitting quietly and enjoying the reality of Your Presence in us. We did not have time to say our personal words of thanksgiving for this greatest of all gifts. But at last we were able to be united to You, and that made it easier. *Deo gratias.*

†††

July 30 – Eucharistic Adoration

At long last today we experienced Eucharistic Adoration for the first time in many weeks. Prior to this we would have Adoration for an entire day from after morning Mass until about 7 p.m., closing with Benediction of the Most Blessed Sacrament. In the interim several of our faithful adorers have passed from this life to eternity, and it was a question of whether or not we could resume our all-day Adoration or perhaps we might begin with a shorter Adoration period. Because we chose to hold Eucharistic Adoration for an hour after morning Mass, several people stayed. Words are inadequate to express the inner joy which comes from simply sitting in silence before Jesus in the Monstrance on the altar. Today, it was like finding a long-lost Friend and just enjoying being in their Presence without needing to say a word. We both know each other so well, and speaking would not give us the words to adequately express the joy we felt. The communication was on the silent level of heart to heart. It was almost like coming home to be with Jesus exposed in the Eucharist. Our pastor has arranged that we will have this Holy Hour every Thursday now – what joy for our hearts!

†††

CRUSHED

My daughter! My husband! My niece! My grandmother! My Uncle!

Oh God, I am crushed beneath the weight of death. The dying are all around me. It does not matter if they are relatives or friends, they have all had a place in my life, and now they are gone. No sweet voices to speak with, no wonderful memories to share. Bits and pieces of me have been chipped away, and the pain is unbearable. Had this dying taken place before this crisis I would be surrounded by hugs and warm consoling words, but now I am alone – no hugs, no phone calls, just this eerie silence of voices I will hear no more. Where are You, my God? Do You see all my sorrow?

Oh yes, You do see my sorrow, the depth of the pain, and the loneliness which has enveloped me like an iceberg in which I am frozen. Yes, You see all this, but I feel so far from You, or perhaps that You are so far from me. No, You can't be far from me because You live within me. Then, we are both frozen and immovable and unable to feel the warmth of compassion which surrounds me. " No", You tell me. " I do feel your pain. I felt it deeply on a Friday, if you remember. I am not distant. It is just that the depth of your pain prevents you just now from comprehending My nearness. I am by your side, holding you up, giving you the strength to face each new and empty day. This is the time when you must really trust in My Presence, even if you cannot sense it. Trust that it is there. Act like it is there, and you will find yourself able to stand. It is true that I am there even in the darkness but remember this: there will always be a dawn. Wait for it."

8.24.2020

†††

THE AGONY OF LOVE

The human soul suffers deeply when the one they love becomes ill beyond the ability of doctors and medicine to heal them. Countless are those who have walked that long lonely road which tears the heart asunder even before their beloved sighs their last sigh. For all the courage and compassion which arises on that road, still, the end of this life for the spouse, child, friend, whoever it may be, is never easy no matter how well we may hold together through the passing and funeral and all the other necessary things which follow immediately. Sooner or later we hit that blank wall. We are confronted not only with the deafening silence, but sometimes the memories of difficult moments come crashing down on us. We face unexpected moments of collapsing in tears. Regrets surface. While we have physically buried the one we loved so much, we find ourselves "buried" in ways we never knew – emotionally, for one, perhaps even confused over the financial situation, or other aspects of daily life.

Our help during this most difficult part of life comes from our closest friends and family members. But through it all, listen. In silence you will hear words to comfort and strengthen you. Day by day, almost unawares, you will slowly move out from under the shadow of death into a new and brighter day. Slowly, but lovingly, you will lay aside the pain and move on to a new life you could not discover until this time. Go gently. Be patient. Time not only heals the deep wounds, it leads us to unexpected horizons and a life we could not have imagined.

LISTENING

Listen to Me

Listen to Me, my child. Attend thine ear always to My Voice. Hear Me in activities around you and be not distracted by the cares of the world. Dare to be sensitive to My inner stirrings. Become so keenly aware of My movement that you will fly in response – not so that you rush to be silent, but that you open your heart sufficiently to understand My directives and then hasten to carry them out.

†††

Gently Be

Gently, gently my child, be thou made gentle in My ways. Look with the eyes of your soul and see the gentleness of Jesus. Feel that gentleness and let it permeate your being. Become My gentlest dove, tenderest of the tender, and feed only on My Love.

†††

Remember

Remember, My child, your task is to keep your eyes fixed on Me. Keep them focused on heaven – your eternal home. You are living in a passing world. Do not be afraid, even if the enemy were to come to your door. Remember always You are My child. As long as you are intent on doing My Will there is nothing to fear. Invoke the saints – remember your guardian angel, but also be very near Our Blessed Mother who can and will keep you safe beneath Her mantle as long as you trust Her. Let Her be your guide and protection. You have nothing to fear.

†††

God from God

True Light from True Light

Because God is Pure Light, nothing containing any darkness can enter the Light. Many souls have experienced "traveling" toward the Light and then returning to their earthly bodies. The Light they experience is beyond description in human words. One man who had a near-death experience said it "is not in our color spectrum" because there were no other words to describe the beauty of that Light. The Light draws souls not just here and now, but most of all upon our death – upon the cessation of our activity in this earthly realm. It has been long held that the essence of who we are lives forever because it resides in our immortal soul. The importance of this is highly significant because only the soul can transcend time and space. As a result of this awareness, one becomes conscious of the importance of keeping one's soul as pure as possible, because only a pure soul can enter the Light. Why? Because to enter the Light is to enter the very Being of God. This is also why the church teaches us that Purgatory exists. It is a place created by the infinite Mercy of God in which our less than perfect souls are prepared and purified for entry into the Eternal Light. That being said, once an earthbound soul comprehends these things it is easily horrified by not just its sins but by any fault which could stain its beauty and delay its final entry into the Heavenly Kingdom.

†††

Thou Art Mine

Come my precious one and leave all this earth's possessions. Come to Me knowing I will care for those you love in the same manner in which I care for you. Place them in My hands and trust them to Me. Entrust them to Me. Depend on Me to care for them. They are also My children. In so doing, you shall gain those gossamer wings on which your soul can fly, and you can bridge the gap between this world and Me by soaring like the eagle on swift and powerful wings. Thou art Mine, my beloved, and I desire that thou wouldst be completely free in this life so we may be enraptured during your sojourn through life.

†††

Don't Worry

Don't worry my child – all is well. You have only to trust in my Divine Providence. You also know that the Heart of Jesus has His own designs for you. You need not run hither and yon. In your peacefulness you will always find Me. Rest in my love.

Sustaining Love

It is not the feelings but your steadfast love which will sustain you in these times. My hand is ever upon you to strengthen you for the days to come. Lean on me always and trust not yourself but My Spirit Who is with you always. Rejoice – even in adversity – for the evil one has no power over my servant who rejoices and praises me in difficulties.

†††

Beloved Child

Beloved child, hear Me. You are where it is My will for you to be. Your love of Me has brought you to a ministry for my priests. Your prayers for them are expressions of your love, not just for them, but for Me. Today you read St. Catherine's words about reverencing Me in my ordained ministers – priests and deacons. It was for this time and place I created you, and I accept your willingness to pray for them. Continue to trust in My providential care. All is well.

†††

THE MINISTRY OF SACRISTAN

Within the church there is a service which lay people can perform, and it is to assist the pastor. Like all vocations, this is one to which a person is called by God. They might not recognize the call at first, but after some time they will understand that this is where God wishes them to serve. It happens slowly, imperceptibly. The author's journey started with prayer, which intensified over time. It included the daily Mass, and God's way of "setting the stage." In the author's case, it started when she was sitting in the last pew of the church and then needed to move forward to lead the Rosary. Step by step, the ministry evolved, acolyte, lector, Eucharistic Minister. Then came the time when I would assist after Mass in putting the Chalice, paten, cruets, etc., away. Along the way came a surprise from one of our parishioners – they gave me a key to the church which they had held for some time and decided I should have it. The next time I saw our pastor, I told him I had been given the key and was willing to return it to him, but he insisted that I keep it. When our pastor retired and the new pastor came, I was asked a simple question: Would you mind opening the church in the morning? I already had the key, so it was obvious to me that I could do that little task. Then, a friend of mine who had been doing some of the after-Mass tasks in the sacristy showed me how to do them. It is amazing to see how slowly and gently God can draw us into forms of ministry we would never have given a thought. Over the years I have learned the sacristan is an important help to the priest because they can open the church, set everything needed for Mass, come to the church at times for funerals or special events, and in short, fills a gap which allows the priest to be more accessible to the parish family. This is a very humbling ministry.

The next time you are at church, you may notice a person who lights the altar candles, puts things on the altar, checks the Tabernacle, makes sure the book of readings is on the right page, etc. These, too, are what a good sacristan does. If you recognize someone in your parish who does these things, thank God that they have answered His call to serve not just the pastor but also the entire parish family.

REDISCOVERING THE HOLY SPIRIT

Everyone knows the Triune God is the Father, Son, and Holy Spirit. Scripture tells us about the foundation of the world, and we read that in Genesis, "the Spirit hovered over the waters." At the moment the angel Gabriel announced to the Virgin Mary the upcoming birth of a son, the Son of God, the "Spirit overshadowed her." When Jesus was baptized in the Jordan River by John the Baptist, "the Spirit descended on Him like a dove." Of course, the most dramatic appearance of the Holy Spirit was at Pentecost when tongues of fire are showered on the Apostles in the Upper Room in Jerusalem. These are the most popular images of the Holy Spirit.

In reading the Scriptures we will come across other references to the Spirit, but they may not make the same impact as the ones cited above. If we pay close attention to the miracles of Jesus, we will see the power of the Holy Spirit effecting miracles at His word. These show us the way God works. Of course, we can easily tell ourselves that these things happened a long time ago and that they do not happen like that today.

There was a time in the United States when a strong movement of prayer engendered a phenomenon very similar to the first Pentecost. These people were called "Pentecostals" because they prayed in strange languages the way the first Apostles prayed in differing languages. We can easily recall that the people who were present when the first Pentecost happened heard the apostles in languages they recognized. Shortly after that we read of a person being healed through the intercession of Saint Peter. The American Pentecostals experienced the same kind of power from the Holy Spirit. After some time, the movement seemed to fade, although there are "Pentecostal" churches still in existence today.

Fast forward to the 1960's, and we find a group of men at Steubenville, Ohio, reading the same Scripture passage about the first Pentecost and wondering why we do not see that kind of power displayed in our time. These men chose to spend a period of time, like a Novena, prior to Pentecost praying earnestly for a new outpouring of the Holy Spirit. On a Pentecost Sunday, these men were gathered together, praying for the coming of the Holy Spirit in the same power as the first Pentecost. To their amazement, they all began to speak in different languages. They prayed for physical healings for some people, and the healings occurred. This "New Pentecost" in the Catholic church made it clear that the Holy Spirit, although not speaking a word, really exists and that this was a manifestation of that "person" in the Blessed Trinity. Two of the men present then were Ralph Martin and Peter Herbeck. Since then, they have spoken at countless religious conferences across the country about these gifts of the Holy Spirit. It is alive and well. There are many books available on this topic, but it is mentioned here because the

Holy Spirit is the "energy" of God which can move us to proclaim Christ's message in these days.

All Catholics receive the gift of the Holy Spirit when they are confirmed, but despite knowing about the gifts and fruits of the Holy Spirit, many people go through life not knowing what these gifts are which they were given, and that it is our responsibility as followers of Christ to know not only about these gifts but to discover which of these gifts have been given to us specifically. Yes, each Catholic receives a certain "charism" or gift from the Holy Spirit, but unless we know what that gift is, it will lie dormant. Hearing God's word to us and responding to this call is enabled when we take the time to pray to know the gifts we have received. Once we know what gifts we have received, then we have a responsibility to use them for the good of others.

The Holy Spirit helps us have a closer relationship with Jesus and also guides us to better follow the Will of God in our lives. During the time when the Holy Spirit seemed to be touching a great many people, there were some things which made people wonder if the Spirit was really behind what they saw or experienced. This was and is a special gift the Spirit would give to some people when there was a gathering to pray for the needs of those assembled. The gift is called being "slain in the Spirit." When this would happen to a person, they would seem to faint, and they would stay in this "faint" for several minutes. It was the strong presence of the Holy Spirit which caused this effect, and frequently, the person who had this experience would find they were healed either emotionally or physically. No one was ever injured when they experienced this touch of the Holy Spirit.

An interesting note to this revelation is that those who would pray for a person who receives this powerful gift of the Holy Spirit would themselves never experience this phenomenon.

At that time in our church history, there were priests who would come to pray at a church for the healing of people. Active members of the Charismatic Renewal would assist the priest in different ways. Some would be assigned to pray with the priest, and others would walk behind a person to catch them in the event they would feel a powerful touch of the Holy Spirit. Did real healings happen? Yes. The author was a prayer partner with a priest at one of these healing Masses. One by one the people would come forward and the priest and myself would pray for the unspoken need of the person. There was a memorable event one time when the person who came for healing told the priest they had a particular need. One of their legs was shorter than the other. The priest asked the person to wait until we finished praying with everyone else, and then he would pray with them.

After everyone had received the prayers they requested, the person with a very unusual request was taken to a separate space where the priest and the author prayed with them. Father held the person's feet in his hands, and his assistant placed their hands above and below the middle of the lower leg. Like this, they prayed for the healing of this person. While they were praying, the assistant could feel the person's leg move through their hands. When the prayers were finished, the person stood up perfectly straight! Miracles are not just things we read in the Bible. They can and do happen even to this day.

Those who were active in these Charismatic Prayer Groups would pray using the "prayer language" given them by the Holy Spirit. The language could not be identified as being from a particular country, but it was a language which lifted the mind and heart of the person praying in such a way that they were fully focused on Jesus. The group of people would pray like this for a while, and then, ever so gently, their voices would become very quiet until everyone was sitting in this profound silence. After a period of silence one of the members of the group would be motivated to stand and share their "word of knowledge" which had been given them by the Holy Spirit. The "word" was usually something which strengthened the faith of all present. These prayer meetings were common for many years, and then they seemed to disappear. While the meetings may have ceased for the most part, the people who participated in these gatherings went on to become more active within their local churches. In that respect, the outpouring of the Holy Spirit years ago helped to build the church from within. Today we need this kind of outpouring of the Holy Spirit to happen in the lives of all who follow Jesus. Like the first Apostles who went from being fearful to unafraid, Catholics and all Christian people need to be strong and confident in speaking about the faith. The church of Jesus Christ is under attack from people who would like nothing better than not to hear about the law of God and the salvation wrought by Jesus Christ. We have seen enough violence and lack of respect for people in many different walks of life. This is not how Jesus would have us live. With the help of the Holy Spirit, all those who follow the teachings of Jesus can make the world a place of peace and good will. Let us all listen to the Holy Spirit and follow in the way He would lead us.

The following list of the gifts and fruits of the Holy Spirit is given so that you may meditate on them and discover for yourself which of these gifts and fruits the Holy Spirit has given to you. Pray to the Holy Spirit to understand how to use these special gifts God has given you.

Seven Gifts of the Holy Spirit: Wisdom, Understanding, Counsel, Fortitude, Knowledge, Piety, and Fear of the Lord.

Fruits of the Holy Spirit: charity, joy, peace, patience, kindness, goodness, generosity, gentleness, faithfulness, modesty, self-control, chastity.

Extraordinary Minister of Holy Communion

Frequently referred to as the Eucharistic Minister, this person assists the priest at Mass with the distribution of Holy Communion. These people are often asked if they would be willing to serve the church and their parish family in this manner, and many people find this a rewarding ministry. For others, the role of Extraordinary Minister of Holy Communion can take them into ministry beyond the church itself. In the author's case, this was not a ministry she had considered. It happened that her neighbor, who was very instrumental in bringing all-day Eucharistic Adoration to our parish, asked one day if she would be willing to become an "EM." At the time of the request, the author was widowed and had recently quit working full time. It was easy to say yes. After being trained, along with several other parishioners, we were commissioned for this ministry. On the very first day of my ministry, one of our deacons came to me after Mass and said he had a parishioner for me to visit. This was not something I anticipated, so with a deep breath, I began the first of a great many visits to homebound parishioners. It was something I enjoyed doing, and the people certainly looked forward to the visit. This ministry was one where I was comfortable, although I never thought of anything beyond serving at church or to whose who could not come to the church. Over the years, however, this ministry has brought me into nursing homes, to hospice, and more recently to the side of people who were dying. By the grace of God and the gifts of the Holy Spirit, I found myself able to assist the families as well as the dying person. Naturally, these were profound, sacred moments. To this day I still marvel at the places and people God has brought me, and the beautiful gift of His spirit at work during those visits.

The Circle of Life

The journey begins in the dark at a time we cannot recall. Here we are imbued with a great many gifts which will surface at different times in our lives. It is as if these capabilities are embedded in the core of our being, unbeknownst to ourselves. Then comes a moment, chosen by God, when we leave the warm, dark world and are suddenly in a cold, bright place. This change of locations is conveniently something we do not have the ability to describe or recall. Many events in our early days are not recorded in our memory because we do not have a language or words to describe that time. This is our first gift – a clean slate – nothing written on it – no blemish or spot – just simply pristine. We have entered this "thing" called time and space. As we grow and learn to walk and talk, to recognize voices and sounds, we also learn a certain word which has been given to us. Our name is something we did not choose – just like the transition from dark to light. We cannot recall when we first heard the word which identifies us and by which we will be known during our time here. Equally curious is the fact that we have no comprehension of where we were before we came here. It is very strange and mysterious, but we know we are loved and cared for and that we belong to those who call us by the name we've been given. And so, the adventure of life begins – without fanfare or notoriety.

For the length of time we have been given for our journey on this strange place called earth, we will, with the help of other travelers, learn many things. We will learn to speak, to walk, to run, to put different words in a group that will make sense to those bigger versions of ourselves. It will be a curious, exciting, and amazing journey. We have arrived in this place unaware that we were created specifically for where we find ourselves, and above all, we are innocent and pure in matters of mind, spirit, and all the facets which will build as we learn more about where we are. Thoughts of the future will elude us for some years, but we will develop capabilities and skills that will become important parts of our lives as they unfold. It is an amazing path on which we have been placed, but we do not see or comprehend it in our beginning.

As our life experiences increase, we tend to think less about where we came from and what we are to do in this life. Eventually, we do come face to face with the decision that will mark a transition from childhood to adulthood. While we may have learned many things along the way, we may not have begun to tap into some of our "hidden" talents. We may discover an interest in science or mathematics or philosophy. We may try physical activities such as baseball or basketball, or football, but as we try these different avenues, we will find an inner sense that this or that direction is not quite what we want to do. However, it is in these attempts at various career choices that we will finally recognize the avenue for which we were created, and when we do, there will be two very important indicators that this is it: we will feel an inner peace about the choice, and we will also find that the more we move in this direction, the greater will be our inner joy. It might even be like one of those "AHA" moments, when we suddenly realize or recognize that this is the way to go. The mystery will be solved, and we will be free to move forward in the chosen direction.

It is not surprising that after many people have worked in a particular occupation, or two, that they discover they have other talents which they did not realize they possessed. Frequently it will be singing, painting, writing, acting, or playing a musical instrument. All of these will not add a deeper dimension to our lives, but they will be able to give pleasure to other people. Here is where we start to move from being so focused on what we want, to thinking of how to make other people happy. It is a great discovery. Sometimes it will be a different shift in which something we learned in our childhood, such as playing a musical instrument which we have put aside, will return and bring joy, happiness, and a sense of accomplishment at being able to share this talent with other people. We will start to look at the world a little differently. Having been on the receiving end of much education, we have now grown to think outwardly toward other people. Church involvement provides many opportunities to be of help in a great many ways. We have become confident and comfortable with who we are and are now ready to move on into the kind of activities that focus on others. High school students sometimes would visit nursing homes and sing for the patients. As we move into and through adulthood, we can become aware of people in need and help in various ways through agencies developed to help the less fortunate. Sometimes we have an opportunity to join an outreach program which helps people in other countries. There are a great many ways to find ourselves helping the needs of our brothers and sisters who are less fortunate than us.

MARKERS along the way.

The journey of our lives is marked with "milestones" many of which are related to our birthdays. It is always wonderful when the day can be marked with celebration. Other milestones along the way are easy to recall: first pet, first day of school, new friends from school, high school with sports, music, drama, and other activities aside from the academics, plus things like making the honors list, or achieving something wonderful while participating in a sports program. All these things contribute to who we are as people and will influence to some degree or another our interests in the future, and most possibly our life careers.

Of course, marriage, is another big marker along the way, as is the birth of the first, or second, or third child. Each of these is a big event. Then there are the other markers – the ones we remember but not with excitement. These are the ones when we lose members of our families or some of our friends. Death puts a shade of gray on days when we remember those who are no longer with us. It is at this time that the gift of friends helps us remain in a better frame of mind, but it also helps us develop a sense of gratitude from having known those people.

There is one marker that is permanent. When we have finished our sojourn on planet earth, we will be called away through a process called death. People do not like death. They prefer life over death, but that marker is unavoidable. What we have learned on our journey, our experiences of seeing people we know and love close the door of this life through the experience of death, all have been a different kind of education. It calls us to think about our own lives. Have we done anything helpful to the people we have met over the years? Have we been the kind of people that other people want to be around? We do not need to be wildly successful at anything in particular. In the end, it is the quality of our life by which we will be remembered.

For many people, the final days of their lives are ones of illness. We are people who do not want to see anyone sick or suffering. It is a part of the overall human nature. The final and most important part of life can come when we see someone in the process of dying. It usually comes gradually, but for others it may come suddenly. Either way, this is the most difficult part of our journey. For people of faith in life after this life, the loss of someone they know is a bit easier because we can hope that they will find their new life better than their last part of life here. But every experience we have with other people is a learning experience. In small ways we learn to understand, to grow more sensitive to certain situations, to know when and what to say when someone is facing the end of their days.

We will never have the answers to all our questions. We will be sad that we will not see some of the people we were close to when they leave this life. But this final marker in life's journey is one we need to address when we become adults. By doing so we will come to understand that we have come to this place with a special gift to share with other people. We are given various experiences to help us understand the complexity of life and appreciate it. All of the hellos and good-byes are markers in our lives as well. The best analogy of life is a tapestry. It is woven from the back side, so the worker does not see the design until it is finished. The strange and hard to comprehend sight of different color threads going in various directions and not creating a pattern is one of the things we are not inclined to think about, but when it is finished and turned over, the results are usually beautiful, and that is how we are to end our lives. It is why we are here in the first place.

And so, from the tiniest of elements we become fully grown humans who learn much during our journey. From beginning to end we spend a great deal of our lives learning all manner of things. When our learning is over, our life completed, we then return to the Source from which we came, and so Life is a Circle. It has a beginning and an end, but they are all one journey, and what we see from here as the end, is just the beginning of another journey. Yes, we will be sad to see someone we are close to leave this life, but remember, this life is the ending of one adventure and the beginning of another one. The human soul never dies. The body in which it resides is its temporary home. One adventure may end, and another begin, but it is all part of a great circle called Life.

Journey's End/Journey's Beginning

A journey in faith does not mean that we do certain things and that's it. Rather, the journey in faith is one which calls us to reach out to others. The most common ways of reaching out are through assistance to food banks, or praying in front of abortion facilities, and many other ways we commonly think of to help others. We also know that praying for each other, or for those in need at times of crisis or health issues, is also a way of living out our faith. We may not think about it too much, but we also express our faith by attending funerals and praying for the deceased. Celebrating the baptism of an infant or adult, is an exciting time in our lives, and we are happy to participate at these sacramental celebrations.

A surprise in our lives might be to find ourselves with someone we know who is in the process of leaving this life and returning to the Source from which we have come. These are not times we tend to look forward to, and perhaps we fear them knowing the time of separation is upon us.

The first dying person I accompanied on their final steps was my own father. We had arranged for hospice care, about which many people are familiar, but not having experienced death up-close and personal before, was something which needed help. The hospice aide was kind enough to provide an information sheet which explained the steps a dying person goes through. This was very helpful to me and all my younger siblings. Our mother was very familiar with death, having experienced the death of her own mother at the age of 50. My mother was about 30 years old.

When our father was dying, the hospice information helped us understand the way the body responds to its imminent end. It is not something to be feared and learning about these steps has proven to be a great asset in the circumstances in which I have found myself on several occasions. Praying as we did when my father died helped him because he could still hear our voices even if he could not respond to us in any way. It also helped us by giving us a greater sense of peace and acceptance. Although he died nearly 30 years ago, that experience was a preparation for the number of deaths I have witnessed since then – both family and members of our church family.

The first time I visited a family with a dying member was a grace-filled time. I knew this family had a great devotion to the Mother of God, so we prayed the Rosary at the bedside of the dying person. God gave me a gift of tremendous compassion for this family and enabled me to provide them with some comfort through the prayers we prayed. Letting go of someone we love is never easy, but I have found that praying around the dying person not only helps reassure them of our love, but it also provides comfort for those who are grieving. Later I learned that the dying person left this earth shortly after I had left the house.

Since that time, I have had the privilege of being with families who are at the point of saying farewell to a member they have known and loved for a long time. On one occasion I found myself grieving for a person I had visited the week before and wondering if I could possibly return to visit them that week.

My grief for this person was profound. I had awakened at 5 a.m. in tears for this member of our parish family. Our pastor reassured me that morning that I would be fine at this visit, and I was – except that when I arrived at the house a week later, the family was gathered in one room, and I was told the family member had passed at 5 a.m. that morning. By the grace of God, I had enough Consecrated Hosts to do a Communion service and prayers with this family. I can only hope that this brought all of them great consolation.

On another occasion I was visiting a dying friend. At this visit I surprised myself by saying a spontaneous prayer shortly before I left. The next day I learned this person had gone to their eternal reward within 30 minutes after I left. I can hear you thinking, you wouldn't want me to visit your house, but these were times of grace. They were times of peace. They were times that gave the family members the gift of letting go of someone they loved so very much. In these settings, we can get a good look at how the Blessed Mother must have felt as she stood beneath the cross on Calvary.

These are the moments which cause us to pause and reflect, not just on the quality of the person's life or what they did, but to reflect on the greatness of God Who gives us the opportunity to be with those we love before they close their eyes on this world and open them in eternity.

Death is not to be feared if we have lived a good, faithful life. The only death to be feared is the sudden, unprepared-for death. Those who have died with their family at their side were blessed up to the final moments. They were surrounded by love and the prayers they all knew so well. I can't think of anything more comforting than that when my last day arrives.

Since I have had the great privilege of being with the dying, one would think that I do this on a regular basis. The only time I find myself with a dying person is when I get a request, as happened not so long ago when a friend's mother was dying. In this case my ministry was to arrange for the anointing of the sick person. After making the arrangements with our pastor for him to visit this person, it occurred to me that many people seem to think that this is something which is given only when a person is dying.

The anointing of the sick is a sacrament, the Sacrament of the sick, and is helpful for us to have the priest pray these prayers for us if we are expecting to go to a hospital, for example, for some surgery. We tend to think of this Sacrament as our last resort for spiritual help, so it is good to remember that this Sacrament is there for many people other than the dying. One parishioner had had a series of repeated health issues. When I asked them how many they had experienced, they said there were four of these events. Then I asked if they had asked for the anointing of the sick. They had not received this Sacrament, and while they were currently in recovery mode, it was apparent that this person could benefit from the Sacrament. Arrangements were made and our pastor and I visited this person. Father prayed the prayers of the anointing, and the parishioner was happy to have these prayers. When I visited them a week or so later, I asked how they felt, and they happily reported they felt significantly better the day after Father had prayed the Anointing of the Sick prayers for them. This does not always happen, and sometimes the person experiences a deeper peace about their circumstances, a sense of acceptance, or a sense that all will be well. It is God Himself who determines what kind of help the person needs most. This is where trust in Him really comes alive.

The ministry to the dying has, in my mind, always been a charism of the priesthood. I never thought of the "lay priesthood" as having great gifts, but we do. The most obvious one is serving as an Extraordinary Minister of Holy Communion, at church and/or to the homebound and those in nursing homes. I have already recounted more than one time when I was with the dying. It has been somewhat of a mystery that I should be with these people and their family, but I must conclude that these are the places where God has called me because despite not being a priest, He has used me to bring comfort to the family and peace to the person who is near the end of their journey here. The most recent experience of being with the dying was with the family of a person I had been bringing Communion to for several months. He had lost his wife several months ago. Now, his family had come from their various locations to be with him. Our pastor had given him the anointing of the sick a week earlier. However, a week later our pastor was not available, and I was moved to call the family and ask if they would like me to come pray with them. They did, and I asked what time they would like me to come. They chose 3 o'clock, the Divine Mercy Hour. When I arrived, we prayed the Divine Mercy Chaplet at the side of this dedicated parishioner who with his wife had been the altar servers at my husband's funeral. When we finished the Chaplet, I offered a set of three prayers for the dying which I have prayed with other parishioners. It was while I prayed these special prayers that this wonderful, generous, faithful parishioner quietly and peacefully slipped the bonds of earth.

The experiences of being with the dying have touched me deeply. I find it extremely humbling to be in the presence of the dying person and their family. It is a very intimate time. By the grace of God, I have had the gift of being able to be in the midst of these delicate people and offer them the help which comes through prayer. My personal experience of being with my mother as my father was dying contributed greatly to my sensitivity to this very precious time when we must say farewell to one we have loved so much and for so long. As I have reflected on these experiences from time to time I am filled with awe and very deep humility at being so privileged to provide comfort to the living as well as the dying. The help of the hospice nurse who attended my father is also a large part of my ability to be incredibly sensitive without bursting into tears myself. Knowing what happens at the end of life helped make it possible for me to be with the dying. They are so fragile, but they also hear. It is true that the sense of hearing is the last sense before the end of life, so it is very important to be attentive and sensitive when we are near a dying person. Everyone reacts differently at such times. There is no way to fully prepare for being at the side of a dying person, but the grace of God comes to our aid. To this day I marvel at the great privilege of being with a family as they bid their final farewell to one of their own. It is not easy, and truly it is the grace of God Himself at this time that makes is possible for me to provide this ministry of prayer and comfort to the living as well as the dying.

In retrospect, considering how gently my own husband passed away, I must confess I was blessed that day to be able to let him go and not to go pieces myself. Through all these years since he left this life, I have had many opportunities to be thankful that being a widow was not the end of my life. In fact, it has turned out to be a new beginning within the church I love, and I am now and probably will be for a long time one who stands in awe of the amazing experiences in my ministry to the members of our parish family. As one good friend said recently, "I am truly blessed." Indeed, I will always be thankful for the manner in which my life changed since the day I kissed my husband good bye. May we all be blessed to have the grace to gently say good-bye to one we love when the time comes and to be thankful for their life with us.

From me to you, I pray that you will know how blessed you are in life, and in the death of someone you love.

A VERY HUMAN CROSS

It was an ordinary day when I was asked if I would be the contact person for a relative who had lost his wife recently and lived alone in a remote part of the country. When I said 'Yes' I would be happy to accept the responsibility, I sensed a heavy weight on my shoulder. Immediately I knew what it was – it reminded me of Jesus' cross. A few months later I received a call from a hospital where this relative was a patient. The doctor who needed to speak with me explained the situation and said this relative could no longer go home or be alone. And so, at their request, this relative came to be with me. In hindsight I was glad we had done the legal paperwork when I was visiting months earlier. Now, the document became very important if I was to take care of this relative.

The day was Christmas Eve when my nieces and a cousin brought this relative to my home. From that day on I was home-bound. For 24 hours a day, 7 days a week, week after week, we were together this, terminally ill relative and me. This was not strange territory. I helped set up home hospice care for my father, and years later for my own husband. I knew the "drill" as one might say. There are probably a great many people who know what these "shoes" feel like. For me, the first good thing was that I knew a lot of people at my church would wonder where I was, and secondly, they would also pray for myself and my relative.

Over the course of the months there have been moments that were trying, and in those moments when I would be tempted to say something unkind, or hurtful, I would find myself checked by the grace of those prayers. It is not easy to care for a person who has difficulty remembering things.

Hospice home care was very helpful, and so, too, was their "respite" program which gave my patient a 5-day break. For 5 days I did not need to care for my relative as they were taken to a hospice facility and cared for there while I had the "luxury" of living a more normal life and doing things which were required to be done outside the home. The most difficult of all things was keeping track of the days. Fortunately, my good friends would call on the telephone and we could talk for a few minutes. Those few minutes were a life-saving device, keeping me connected with the world outside. As I write this, I am still caring for this member of my family.

Every morning when I wake up, I sit quietly and wait for this family member to stir. They do not get up at the same time every day, and there have been mornings when I would be sitting at a table facing the direction of the bedroom, waiting, and waiting, and watching the clock, and waiting. All the while the thought runs through my head: will they get up on their own this morning, or will they have slipped away during the night?

This, I have found, is where trust in God plays a very important role. If I did not have faith and trust in God, I would be the proverbial "basket case." However, the gift of patience is rewarded when this relative opens the door and says good morning. Not knowing when a person will breathe their last breath is very stressful, but we have no way of knowing, and God does not make it a habit of telling us.

Frequently, along the way, I have been reminded of Jesus' painful struggle on His way to Calvary, and that has been a source of strength as well as encouragement to recommit myself to caring for this family member.

Today I write this, grateful for all the prayers and spiritual support which have been with me on this journey. My pastor and Deacon have been kind enough to bring me Holy Communion. Members of the parish family call from time to time, and knowing I have those resources has made this a much easier journey than it might have been.

To all those who know what it is like to care for someone who is terminally ill, you have been chosen for this task. God has given you the strength and patience to endure as well as the grace to let go at the end and commend your loved one into His arms. In the very end of it all, enabling someone we love to leave this world peacefully is a tremendous gift. While we may weep and mourn, let us remember that there comes a time when we must give back to God the gift He has given us in this person. May your souls be filled with peace knowing that in caring for your family member or friend, you have been caring for Jesus Himself.

Fiat Voluntas Tua

†††

LOOKING FORWARD

Since becoming an Extraordinary Minister of Holy Communion, I have had the privilege of serving our parish family not only at Mass in church, but also when I come to their homes to bring them Eucharist. One morning the substitute priest did not arrive in time for morning Mass. Our pastor was contacted, and he gave me permission to do a service which included distribution of Holy Communion. I used the same prayers we use when visiting home-bound parishioners but included the readings for the day. We also used the prayers for the faithful as we usually do. The same words were prayed before the reception of Holy Communion, and then everyone came forward to receive the Eucharist. The same prayers I used when visiting the home-bound were used to conclude our prayers that morning.

Following this unexpected Communion celebration, I began to think more about the shortage of priests and what might be done to assist our pastors and parishes. This need and how to address it became the focus of many reflections. This new assistance took the form of Eucharistic Pastoral Minister. That means that those who were commissioned as Extraordinary Ministers of Holy Communion would be capable of assisting the pastor in more ways than assisting at the Liturgy. It was envisioned to be another level of ministry, and these people would be commissioned for this service to the church, but not by the pastor – by the bishop. It would clearly define their service to the church as above that of simply distributing Communion at Mass or to the homebound. Their ministry would be expressly to assist the pastor who has no other ordained priest or deacon for support.

For a long time, I had been thinking about the need in our church and how to address it. The title of the position was of paramount importance because it would give an indication of the role this person would serve in the local church. The term "pastoral" indicates that these people would help shepherd the local church since the needs of the parish cannot be met by one priest. This "layer" of additional help should be able to attend to the more basic needs within the parish and allow the pastor to better utilize his time for liturgical, administrative, and prayer needs. The health of the pastor is contingent on all of these. In addition to assisting with the ministry at the church, these people would also be trained to do pastoral visiting to nursing homes and hospitals and interface with the pastor for the sacrament of the sick and/or reconciliation. With the decreasing clergy population, both priests and deacons, a void has developed in terms of enough clergy to meet the needs of a large parish of 2,000 people or more.

The term Eucharistic Pastoral Minister is designed to allow expanded service from Eucharistic ministers and to avoid confusion in their expanded service to the church. For this reason, these people would be commissioned by the Bishop expressly to assist the pastor who has no other ordained priest or deacon for support.

For an average size parish, 4 Eucharistic Pastoral Ministers would seem to be appropriate. This way the ministry can be rotated since all these people would be volunteering their service to the church.

In writing this reflection on the need for additional help for our pastors and deacons, I suddenly realize that at various times the ministry I have personally provided has been what I have described in this new ministry for the church. In reading through my notes on this proposed new ministry for the Catholic Church, I have documented the variety of services I have provided to some of our parishioners.

Whether or not this proposal becomes implemented is at the discretion of the local Bishop with the help of the Holy Spirit. For those readers who have questions or would like to submit a comment, send them to raydiance1@Comcast.net and put Eucharistic Pastoral Ministry in the subject line.

Made in the USA
Middletown, DE
23 April 2022